"Terri Hewitt's story is an amazing testimony of God's supernatural love and deliverance. In her darkest moments the Lord's arm was not too short to save. Her powerful story will encourage you in whatever situation you may be in and stir your faith to see the hand of God moving in your own life."

Ché Ahn
President of Harvest International Ministry
Senior Pastor, Harvest Rock Church

Terri shares very honestly both the pain and the process of rebuilding after a trauma. In recounting her story she is able to put into words the grief, numbness, confusion, and doubts that she experienced in those early days and weeks. This book will be very helpful for others who experience trauma, and perhaps even more for their loved ones who seek to uphold them and understand some of what they may be experiencing. As I read the book I felt as if I was walking with her through this time - experiencing with her the wonder of God's healing touch and restoration. Through it all, the love and tenderness of God is clearly seen. So that by the end we can echo Terri's call: "Climb with me and hold on to the Rock which saves!"

Dr. Betty Sue Brewster,
Associate Professor of Language and
Culture Learning, Fuller Seminary

THE ROCK
WHICH SAVES

Written By TERRI HEWITT
Illustrations By RIVER CHEN

DEDICATION

~ ✢ ~

I dedicate this book to the "riches of His glory" in Jesus Christ. His amazing grace, never ending love, and great power can save and deliver us all!

"I will present my thank offerings to You.
For You have delivered me from death and my feet from stumbling, that I may walk before God in the light of life."

Psalm 56:12b-13

TABLE OF CONTENTS

~ ✦ ~

"If God causes you to suffer much, it is a sign that He has great designs for you, and that He certainly intends to make you a saint. And if you wish to become a great saint, entreat Him yourself to give you much opportunity for suffering; for there is no wood better to kindle the fire of holy love than the wood of the cross, which Christ used for His own great sacrifice of boundless charity."

— St. Ignatius of Loyola

ACKNOWLEDGMENTS

~ ✛ ~

I have been extremely blessed with many wonderful people who have been supportive and encouraging throughout the entire episode of the avalanche, the healing process, and the writing of this book.

First of all, I am deeply indebted to Josh Colp who unburied me with his bare hands from the thousands of rocks which surrounded me. He sat by my side throughout that dreadful and horrific night on the mountain, praying and encouraging me all along the way.

I am greatly appreciative for all the love, support and hours of talks on the phone with my family, especially my mother, and my "adopted" parents, Bob and Ruth Squires. Your love and sacrificial time given over those many difficult, yet healing months has been invaluable to me!

I am grateful for all the personal help, care and support from all of those who worked at SRAM--for Vincent, Peter and Judy, and especially for Samuel, Joanne, Cherry, Maggie, Jane, Jack, Elbert, Eric, Harry, Darren, Jeffrey, Stanley, Jason, George, James, Silvia and Kay. Each of you has been a special support and friend to me in each of your own ways.

I thank all the staff at Banner Church who prayed me through "my burial experience" and interceded on my behalf for God's deliverance that night up on the mountain. I thank you for visiting and praying with and for me, and showing your love and care. Thank you especially Pastor Samuel and Pastor May, Stephen and Sebina, Vincent's wife, Maggie, Linda, Bonnie and my Friday night Bible study group (I couldn't have imagined a more powerful prayer time!).

With gratefulness, I thank all the members on my Western team of teachers working in Taichung. Your prayers, love and support were deeply felt. Stephanie, Amanda and Carrie— your help especially those initial weeks off the mountain was much appreciated.

Last but not least, I am very thankful for my three precious and dear friends who were my editors for this book. Tom, you're the one who helped me get started, plug away at this book and never give up! Your constant array of questions for me to elaborate on in my monthly manuscripts was awesome! I can't thank you enough for your many months' worth of help. Ruth, your grammar corrections, rereading and rewording of my endless redundancy was invaluable! And Elliot, your ceaseless care for words, the right metaphors and motifs used, as well as paragraph and chapter breaks, was amazing! Working with you was an awesome experience and I'm deeply obliged to you! Thanks you three! And thanks River for your beautiful and amazing illustrations…they're beautiful.

Thanks to each one of my friends from my California churches who wrote me countless letters, sent encouraging scripture passages and have supported me throughout these last couple years. Your love, friendship and prayers have been priceless. Thank you my dear friends! I am truly touched!

PREFACE

~ ✛ ~

First of all, I would like to thank my co-workers and friends at SRAM for all their support which I have received these past three years. In no way have these experiences which I write about in this book affected or changed my view of the company's integrity, safety and commitment to me and their employees. The events you are about to read were unforeseen and unexpected. It was a tragic accident that three precious lives were lost. Everyone in the company, managers and employees alike, all mourn for Keiko, Lawrence, Clive and their families. The sole purpose of this book is to honor God and to reveal that though tragedies do occur in life, we can, by God's grace and strength, pull together and rise above life's challenges.

PART I: Rocked

"When My World Was Rocked"

The Avalanche

May is considered one of the rainiest months of the year in Taiwan. Often times, the rain comes down with sudden outbursts and downpours. Other times, however, it rains continually for days or weeks, and in May of 2005, it was no different. The rain during that month came down at a steady, persistent rate for days on end. It continually poured forth and was unrelenting in its barrage of power. The sky was always darkened and the grayness of the environment was felt not only outside, but also from within our four walls.

During this time, SRAM, the bicycle company at which I teach English to the engineers, was planning another annual hiking trip in May. I had come to Taiwan in December 2003 to do my thesis work for my Master's degree in Teaching English to Speakers of Other Languages (TESOL) and upon my arrival to Taichung, Taiwan, I got the job at SRAM. I finished my thesis within the first six months and due to enjoying my work there, I decided after my graduation from Azusa Pacific University, I would return to Taichung and resume my job after the summer. I continued working at SRAM and participated in the various activities they offered such as biking trips and hiking trips. In the past years they had gone hiking to places like Jade Mountain, Snow Mountain and, in 2004, Jamin Lake.

Since I had just arrived at SRAM six months before, I had the opportunity to go on their trip to Jamin Lake which ended up being an extremely strenuous hike for me. Though the hike had granted one of the most spectacular views I have ever seen, grand mountain peaks set with a backdrop of crystal clear blue skies, the climb up to these summit pinnacles of Taiwan was one of the toughest ascents I had ever made. However, the expedition in 2005, was supposed to be a relatively easy climb in comparison to the hikes taken in prior years and even children were invited to join. It was considered easier because the ascent was gradual and only approximately 12 kilometers (7.5 miles) one way would be hiked. The plan was to go to Tun Yuen Mountain, located in Nantou County near Puli on May 12th and hike the first five kilometers (3 miles) and then stop for lunch at a base camp. We would then resume the hike for seven kilometers (4.5 miles) up Chi-Lai Mountain where we would stay the night at another mountain cabin shelter.

The path we intended to climb was supposed to be a hiker's paradise. The road was sheltered under large pine trees and was approximately six feet wide, broad enough that even a scooter with a wagon carried behind could drive up the gravel road to transport items others might need. The Japanese had constructed this road nearly 60 years ago as a cross-island road and built it to move troops and supplies across Taiwan rather than along the island shoreline.

For weeks and months prior to any hiking trip, numerous arrangements need to be made. For our group, these included finding experienced guides to lead us over the rocky terrain of Taiwan, obtaining permits from the police to go into the mountains, finding accommodations, making food prepara-tions and determining who will carry it. The preparations for this trip were no different, yet as the days were approaching for our departure time, Taiwan was having another rain storm. It rained nearly every day for a week preceding our planned hike on May 12th. I remember thinking to myself over and over again whether the company would still go ahead with this hiking trip as scheduled. I was starting to feel anxious and in order to calm myself down I called one employee, Sam, for more information since he was one of three contact people designated for this trip. As a contact person, he could field our questions or inform us of changes. It was two days before the departure date on Thursday and I asked him what things I needed to pack for our journey. He told me that I needed to wrap all items in extra plastic bags in my backpack to prevent things from getting wet. I also needed to bring a good raincoat.

I remember I was extra busy that week; I was teaching more hours and cramming five days of classes into three since I would be taking Thursday and Friday off for the hike. While I was packing for the trip, I kept telling myself to pray about whether I should be going on this hike. Whether the outing is small or large, I usually ask God if in fact I should be involved or not. I pray a simple prayer, "God if you want me to do this, you lead me. I ask that you would silence the devil's voice and silence my voice and its will, in the name of Jesus. I ask in Jesus' name, should I in fact do this or not, yes or no?" I usually wait for a moment and try to discern what I feel more peace about or what my spirit is more inclined towards. If I feel more tranquility or a stronger sense of the answer being yes, I do it. If I feel a strong sense of no, then I will not do it. This time, however, I was so distracted with my heavier workload of classes and teaching and packing, that I simply did not take those few necessary minutes to be still before God and pray.

As I was preparing my bags, I kept recalling how I hated trudging in the rain and I hoped it would not rain during our three-day hike. But since I viewed this outing, like every trip I took with the people of SRAM, as an opportunity to be with them, befriend them and get to know them better, I simply packed my bags and got ready to go. In the past, the outings with these people had always been enjoyable and full of times for deeper friendship-building.

In the past, on trips with SRAM, I was usually the only foreigner. This time, however, a few other foreigners would be joining us. A Canadian fellow teacher with me at SRAM, named David, was coming. Kai-Ube, a German engineer working as the director of SRAM in Suzhou, China, would be in Taiwan that week. Josh, a friend of mine, was one of a group of teachers that had arrived at the end of January from the United States to join my team serving with a Taiwanese church, Banner Church. Since joining Banner, he had recently gotten to know some of SRAM's Christian employees who were members of Banner, so I asked him if he would be interested in joining us on this hiking trip. He readily agreed since he was interested in getting more involved in biking and doing triathlons.

On Thursday, May 12th, Josh and I met at approximately 5:30 A.M. to ride our motorbikes together up to the SRAM office. I remember it was just barely sprinkling, but I hoped deep within it would stop soon.

"So are you all packed and ready to go?" Josh asked me.

"I suppose," I said, "but I just wish the rain would stop for good. I'm thankful it's not pouring right now, but I sure don't want it to start up again."

"Oh, it's not that bad to hike in the rain," Josh said, "Haven't you done it before?"

"No," I answered, and I was still secretly hoping not to experience a hike in the rain.

We made it to the office at 5:45 A.M. and as people began arriving, we were greeted and given a little packet of food for the day's hike. It included an apple, a couple of granola bars, and some rehydration packets to add to our water.

Around 6:30 A.M., we loaded into the bus. Josh and I sat next to each other and talked nearly the entire ride to our destination. The drive was beautiful! It was nice to get out of the city and start seeing open fields of rice paddies and greenery all around. We traveled over an hour north along the highway before we made our final ascent, and made a quick stop at a breakfast shop and a 7-11, the local convenient store in Taiwan which seems to be located at nearly every corner of every city. I got a rice packet with some tuna inside, as well as a diet Coke since I am hypoglycemic and need lots of regular little protein boosts. We were on the road again shortly and we began our steady ascent up the windy road into the beautiful mountains, reaching our destination around 9:00 A.M.

When we got up from our seats, I remember watching people make last-minute adjustments on their backpacks, arranging who would carry what food, what clothes to wear, and how to pack the important rain gear on top, in case of rain. Sam then asked me, "Do you have a Bible?"

I said, "Of course, why?"

A friend had just texted him on his cell phone about a Bible verse and he wanted to look it up. In the last month, Sam had started going to an "English club" which emphasized biblical principles and he was just becoming interested in learning more about Christ. Little did we all know that this trip would be life-changing for both of us, leaving Sam forever changed by the power and might of God.

Unfortunately, Sam was not able to look up that Bible verse, for just after I responded to him, we were all called outside in order to get going on our hike.

The weather was fairly clear; the clouds had lifted and there was even a little sunshine. We took group pictures and were given brief instructions before starting our hike. Since the guides were Taiwanese and only spoke Chinese, we foreigners, Josh, David, Kai-Ube, and I, all gathered around Vincent and Peter, the managers of SRAM, for translation. We heard then how the Japanese had made this road and why they made it.

Around 9:30, we started making our way up the road. At first it was a paved road up the mountain, but within fifteen minutes we were on the gravel trail which led to the top of the mountain. Although the road that traversed the mountain was very wide, the first 400 meters of it were completely covered in rocks. The mountain at this place was barren and void of greenery; all that was before our eyes were thousands of fallen rocks and pebbles. An avalanche or landslide had fallen recently from the top of the mountain, blocking our six-foot wide trail. Fortunately, however, someone had cleared a new walking path about eighteen inches wide to the other side of the fallen rocks, so we could continue.

Our group of thirty-eight people, including Kimmy, the ten-year-old daughter of Jack, a SRAM employee, hiked in single file. For approximately a quarter-mile, we walked on this narrow, make-shift trail one by one, and made it to the other side of the fallen avalanche area to find our road was again about six feet wide.

When we arrived at this main road, I looked up and saw the many trees, which were above us, all around. There could not be any avalanche in this area since the vast amount of trees and their root system held the soil intact, preventing the mountain's earth from being uprooted and falling. The little road we had just traversed was desolate and treeless, so it was no wonder the earth had given way and there was an avalanche there. We were under trees now and hopefully under their protection from rain and possible landslides.

As we crossed bridges beneath tall mountain waterfalls and followed the ridge trails, sometimes with vertical drop-offs of 200 feet, we were stunned by the enormity of the mountains and cliffs. The sights were spectacular and awe-inspiring, yet, due to the massive cliffs, I also felt nervous chills down my spine. It all made me feel exceptionally small in comparison to these heights and depths.

Within 45 minutes, it began to rain and we all tried to take shelter under the towering trees, grabbing our rain gear out of our backpacks. Our stop didn't take too long, but when we began hiking again, it started to rain—hard. Unfortunately, from that moment on, for the duration of our hike, it never stopped raining for long.

Thankfully, around noontime we arrived at our first destination, the little mountain house called base camp. In the first room we shed our raincoats. In the second room, further into the house, most of us sat down to drink our hot tea or coffee and eat our noodle soup. Beyond these rooms was the kitchen where our lunch had been prepared. Finally, beyond the kitchen and to the side of it, were two rooms for sleeping quarters.

Around 1:00 P.M., despite the heavy rainfall, we all gathered our bags and ventured outside for the remainder of our day's hike. It was just a few hours more till the second mountain house where we would stop for the night, eat and sleep.

I walked and talked with various people along the way throughout the journey upward, but most of the time, I stayed with Josh and chatted with him. After an hour into this second part of our hike, without warning, I noticed that the people ahead of me were congregating at a particular place. Most everyone was speaking excitedly in Chinese.

"Do you see that gorge?" asked one.

"I've never seen this kind of ravine before," said another.

"Nature is so powerful. I can't believe it can wash away such a big area," said yet another.

Our road had come to an abrupt end because evidently a huge landslide had recently occurred. A large gorge now existed between the road we were standing on and the road which we needed to cross. The roads were completely separated by about 100-200 meters and there was no way of crossing since the landslide had obviously come barreling down the mountain and huge trees and rocks now lay in the ravine below. We were unable to proceed forward so we all slowly began retracing our steps back down, and I kept wondering and thinking to myself what we were going to do now.

~ ✛ ~

As we made our way back down the mountain, I heard the people up ahead of me say we were going to walk down to the original mountain house we had stopped at for lunch, discuss what our options were, and proceed from there. As we talked back and forth during that next hour, I heard rumors that maybe we would hike all the way back down to the bus, and drive to a hotel in the nearby mountain grassland area of Ching Jing which had a hot spring and spend the night there. Honestly, at that point, I was getting sick of the rain and the prospect of a warm shower and a warm bed sounded enticing!

When we all finally did arrive back at the mountain house, the rain had subsided and we were able to gather outside on some little benches and listen to the various options the SRAM managers proposed. Vincent and Peter told us we could hike back down to the bus, call it a day, drive back to Taichung and have our regular weekend back at home; or we could descend and stay the night at the hotel with a spa. For a group of thirty-eight people, to switch plans and come to a consensus was not easy. After 30-45 minutes, we all as a group decided to go to the spa for the night. I think all of us were glad that this trip would not come to an end and we would in fact enjoy ourselves at the hotel and spa.

The managers released us to go down the mountain and some people literally took off running down the mountain, probably to get some "real exercise" since our weekend hiking excursion no longer existed. Among those running down the mountain were Kai-Ube, Alan, an engineer in Taichung, Judy, the third manager (along with Peter and Vincent), and Josh. The four of them ran down together and made it quickly to the end of our trail.

I ended up walking the rest of the way down the mountain with a Taiwanese lady, Bonnie, whom I knew at Banner church in my Friday night Bible study, which I had started four months prior in January. We talked extensively about our families, how we became Christians, and the work of God in our lives. The two-hour hike down to the bus flew by as we shared stories from our lives.

However, while we walked down the spacious trail, sometimes I would walk close to the trail periphery to look down at the 100-200 foot drop-offs. It stunned me that we could walk so close to the rim without there being any protective barrier or hand guard along the path, but I couldn't help feeling fascinated by the drop-offs. As I gazed down, though, the dangerous height scared me and I tried to stay in the middle of the path or closer to the mountain side of the road as Bonnie and I talked.

Around 4:00 in the afternoon, we rounded a bend and saw our bus. What a lovely sight! The rain had stopped and started several times during our walk down, and the prospect of getting into a warm cozy environment was all the more exhilarating. Though I love hiking, I was so excited to climb aboard that bus, take off my wet socks and shoes, and start warming up. I was actually glad to end this hike, get out of the rain, and especially get out of my wet clothes. In an attempt to stay warm, I had on underneath my raincoat, a t-shirt, a turtleneck, and a light coat. Unfortunately, now I was not only wet on the outside from the rain, but I was wet on the inside as well due to all the perspiration over the course of our two-hour walk.

As Bonnie and I came around the bend, there was another congregation of people gathered. A new avalanche or land-slide had just fallen in front of our path. The eighteen-inch footpath we had crossed that morning was now completely blocked. Since it had rained nearly all day long, the soil had become saturated, and it seemed it couldn't help but trigger the rocks and land to be dislodged and fall downward, causing the avalanche.

Getting to the other side of it was not going to be easy. Many rocks had fallen making a slope of about a 45-degree angle of stones. Since our final destination was the bus that could so easily drive us all down from the mountain and out of the rain, we spoke eagerly about what plan of action would enable us to cross to the other side. Many more people who had been behind Bonnie and myself began to arrive and join the discussion in Chinese. Unfortunately, just ten to twenty feet in front of our former path was a large vertical drop-off.

If and when we did cross, we would need to go upwards so as to avoid that drop-off.

Within a few minutes of our arrival, Bonnie mentioned that we would probably need to hike back to the mountain house we had come from two hours before and spend the night there. I was stunned. Our bus was in sight less than a quarter of a mile away. How could we possibly turn around, hike all the way back up to that house in the pouring rain, and stay the night? Where did she get this idea from? Had she heard this suggestion from someone else or was this her own idea? When I asked her about it many months later, she told me when she mentioned it, it was just her own idea. At the time, however, I never asked her why she said this, since it was an idea I really didn't want to hear, nor was I willing to swallow.

I decided to move to the front of the crowd where I could hear English being spoken; Josh and Sam were talking about how they could construct a path upwards, away from the drop off.

"Hey Sam, I was thinking, if we try to make a path that goes up and across the mountain, we could try to get over to the other side," said Josh.

"Yeah," replied Sam, "we could try. But how are we going to do that?"

"I've heard of landslides happening near my hometown, in Santa Barbara," answered Josh, "and they could be traversed by just going up to a higher level before crossing. Each person has to plant his feet deep into the mud, so they won't slip though."

"Yeah, it's really muddy, wet and rocky," replied Sam. "But I think we can do it. Let's give it a try."

I stood by their sides watching and waiting to see what they would do. Josh and Sam climbed upward but it was no small feat. With each step, they needed to grab onto anything hanging down. At first, they saw a tree with its branches caught in the midst of the mudslide and since the branches were hanging down low enough, they made it easy for Josh and Sam to grab onto. As they continued to climb upward, they noticed a cable coming down that was suspended from somewhere up in the mountain. They grabbed onto that to further support themselves. The cable provided extra leverage and support for them to go up and walk across the avalanche. By this time, several more gathered around and watched them rig up this path up and across the fallen rock.

Because I did not understand too much Chinese, I did not know what the guides were saying. In fact, I do not remember them stepping out from the crowd and giving us direction, but after talking personally with Vincent months later, and asking specifically how we all decided to take our final course of action, he told me that the guide did talk with both Vincent and Peter at that critical moment. He agreed that going up and over the avalanche could be done and would not be too difficult. Vincent told me that he, along with the guide, realized he and probably the other men could climb up and over, but he was concerned about the women and Jack's child, Kimmy. Peter and he decided that the group could cross over and within a certain time frame, 45 minutes before nightfall, they would re-evaluate and see how many people had indeed crossed.

As I stood watching Sam and Josh, I felt determination rising within me to get across and, in fact, to show the others that it could be done. However, I never thought through logistically that bringing thirty-eight people over would take a long time and each individual would have to muster his or her own courage and strength to get across. Of course, some might be adamantly opposed, but I never thought through these things. I just wanted to get across! The bus was clearly in sight, we had walked all day in the rain, and it was after 4:00 P.M. Since dusk would soon be approaching, getting to the other side into the bus and to a warm hotel beckoned me to proceed.

After Josh and Sam had carefully completed a make-shift path, they needed volunteers to climb up and over the avalanche area. I volunteered first. The cable to grab onto was rough and hard to grip.

"Terri, take out your gloves," yelled someone, "the ones you were given this morning. Use those to grab onto the cable. It'll make it easier to climb upward."

I opened my backpack, found the gloves, put them on and put my pack on again. I steadily made my way upward. It was tricky though since it was on an ex-tremely slippery muddy slope. Josh and Sam had found a couple other dangling cables and while they held onto those, and I held onto my cable, they helped push me upward until I finally made it to a higher place where I could walk across. I had to firmly dig my feet into the mud, as they instructed and lean into the mountain in order to cross. After I made it to the other side, slowly others started to follow me. However, the rain started coming down again, and with that, the soil became more unstable. Some big rocks like the size of basketballs started whirling down the mountain, yet thankfully no one was in their way.

The climb upward along the cables was quite difficult for each person so a new plan was put into action. One of the hiking guides found a large piece of wood, about 20 feet long and two feet wide, and it was laid horizontally across the mountain where the path had once been. The guide also had a long rope and while he held onto it with several men alongside of him, he threw the rope to the other side of the wood plank, where Josh, Lawrence, a SRAM employee who had just crossed the avalanche from up above, tried to catch it.

Unfortunately, when Josh was trying to catch the rope, he slipped and slid down the mountain about 10 feet. Vincent and Bonnie told me later that when they saw Josh slide downward, at that moment several rocks fell from the avalanche above us all, and literally bounced and rolled right past and over him. Josh himself said he never knew about the bounding rocks, but just scrambled and climbed back up to the place where everyone else was standing. But Vincent said from that moment on, fear began to sink into his heart.

The guide then instructed everyone to walk across the wood plank and hold onto the rope while people on both sides held firmly onto the rope, thus keeping it taut and acting as a sort of handrail for those who crossed.

One by one, a couple of girls began to cross and I remember specifically watching one girl, Keiko, an employee at SRAM and one of my English students, lose her footing. She immediately grabbed hard onto the rope and all the men on both sides pulled tightly to keep it firm, without any slack in the rope. As they braced it for her, she gradually made it over safely.

After about 45 minutes, only ten people had crossed. There were still over 20 people on the other side and I thought to myself, this was going to take a really long time. I started to pray and kept thinking, "Can we all really do this?"

Doubt started to creep into my heart and I was beginning to feel nervous. I began to walk down towards the bus and noticed that around the next bend, there was yet another small avalanche to traverse. It could be crossed, but nevertheless it was also dangerous. I walked back to the group when suddenly Judy approached me from behind and urged me strongly to come with her down off the mountain to the bus. She, as well as Kai-Ube, had arrived down the mountain first since they had run down after we were told we would now be going to Ching Jing Farm. Though the avalanche had already fallen when they arrived, they did make it across. She and the wife of one of the guides wanted to now go down to safety.

I remember looking to the right towards the bus and then looking left to the group. To the right was the muddy, slippery and still dangerous trail to the bus. To my left were the other 20 plus people on the other side of the avalanche. I had this deep urgency to pray for them and I felt deep within, I could not leave them. I thought that if I kept my eyes on them, I would pray for them more so. I did not say any of this to Judy, but instead I only said to her, "No, you go on ahead." She was gone within minutes and made it down safely along with the guide's wife and Kai-Ube.

As I gazed back upon the large group, I saw Jack across the way holstering his daughter up on his back, and I nearly screamed out loud, "No, don't do that!" For some reason I felt vehemently opposed to him crossing that rickety wood plank with his daughter Kimmy on his back. Two times I watched him put her on his back and then remove her. I kept praying and crying out in my heart, "No, No!" At last, on his third attempt, he gave up and stopped. Later on, he told me that every time he picked her up, he just could not do it. It was as if a force was preventing him from carrying out his plan. He said he had carried her easily many times in the past, but this time simply could not. I knew when he told me this that it was definitely the hand of God, which prevented him from moving forward. God had truly protected them both!

The rain had been falling on and off for the last hour and now as it started up again, the ground above us was saturated. Suddenly the soil and rocks began to move rapidly downward. Some huge boulders started rolling down the mountain and once that began to happen, we knew it was no longer safe for anyone else to cross. At any moment a rock could come flying down the mountain, and, if anyone was trying to cross at that moment, it would be dreadful. Vincent told me later that at this moment he called his wife Maggie and asked her to start praying for us. He sensed we were in grave trouble and we really needed help and prayer.

The rain intensified and at that time Alan, one of the four who had run down with Judy and Kai-Ube, approached Josh. Apparently, Alan had yet to go down to the bus, and he asked Josh to assist him down over the other small avalanche on the other side of where we were all standing. Josh and he went down together and while he was at the bus this time, Josh told Judy and Kai-Ube, that we really needed help. The nine of us in the group were in an unsafe place, as well as the other twenty-four on the other side and darkness was imminent. Josh was given a high-powered flashlight, and then he ran back up the hill, crossed the avalanche once more and came to join the nine of us: one guide, Sam, Arthur, Clive, Lawrence, Lina, Keiko, Shaowsy, and myself, now caught between two avalanches.

When Josh headed down to the bus with Alan, I was standing and talking with Clive and Lawrence. Both of them were recent students of mine at SRAM and had been in my class for about three months. Both of them were very kind men and studied English hard. As the three of us watched Josh and Alan steadily go across the small avalanche without any sort of assistance of ropes or trees, make it to the other side and begin their descent, Clive turned to me and said he was really anxious to get off this mountain. He told me his wife was expecting a baby. I was so surprised because I did not even know he was married, so I asked him about it. He told me he had been married five months earlier and his wife was now four months pregnant. He wanted to get back down to her.

As Josh reappeared, I made up my mind along with Clive, we should do the same thing as Alan. It would be scary to cross another avalanche, this time without any sort of assistance from cables, ropes or trees, but since I was becoming uneasy about our situation, and we saw Alan and Josh accomplish the exploit successfully, I felt we could do it, too. I was beginning to feel the tension in my heart mounting and felt stronger and stronger that our situation was not safe and we needed to get off that mountain.

After Josh came back alongside of us, I mentioned we should try to go down, too. I had barely uttered the words from my mouth, when suddenly the guide was speaking and telling our group of ten that we needed to stay right where we were and not to move anymore. He spoke firmly in Chinese and only after someone translated it for Josh and me, I noticed how the others were responding to him and I realized that is what we had to do.

I surveyed the area and realized we had very little ground to stand upon. We all faced outward, with our faces towards the cliff and the mountain behind us. To our left was the avalanche we had just crossed with our group of twenty-four on the other side standing in a relatively safe area since the road was wider with many trees above. To our right was another avalanche, which was now beginning to fall. Little rocks about the size of our hands and sometimes the size of a basketball would come crashing down over there. We saw that we were now trapped between two landslides and darkness was approaching.

Someone in our group decided we needed to call the police and, I remember, we kept using Keiko's phone. Keiko was also a recent student of mine and in class was always smiling, friendly, and helpful. Here she was again being accommodating and letting us use her phone.

Several times the police called us back in order to assess our situation more carefully. But again, due to a lack of clear translation, I could only gather bits and pieces of the dialogue with the police. They wanted to know our exact location, yet it also appeared they might not be able to get a helicopter to us. We just needed to wait. I started becoming frustrated and said something like, "Do the police understand this is an emergency?"

I was beginning to sense the gravity of our situation and that something urgently needed to be done quickly. Yet, while we were calling, on the other side, Vincent and the guide were also calling the police and asking for assistance and trying to urge them to come up Tun Yuan mountain.

The ten of us were standing side by side when suddenly we felt a rumbling beneath our feet and heard a roar like the sound of thunder. Some of the people in our group ran for whatever cover they could find. There was a cement wall, about six feet wide and three feet high. A few people ran towards that wall to try to duck in front of it for safety; a few others tried to run in the other direction towards the avalanche, which we had just crossed. Since Clive, Lawrence, and I had people on our right and people on our left when we heard the noise, we just backed ourselves up towards the mountain and placed our bodies in a very slight crevice in the mountain.

Within seconds, as the sound became louder and louder, I suddenly looked up and saw a massive movement of rocks from the mountain hurling down upon us. It was as if a hundred thousand little rocks were moving in slow motion, coming as one big onslaught towards us. I remembered that in elementary school we were taught that if a big earthquake was coming, we were to get in a crouched position, duck our heads, and shield our heads with our arms and hands.

I had been standing upright when I saw the massive flow of rocks, yet instantly I responded and started to bend my legs into the crouched position and move my arms upward towards my head. I ducked my head and buried my chin into my chest.

But within seconds I was completely buried by the rocks.

I never felt the rocks filling up first at my feet, then my torso, and lastly my head. It happened so fast that I was instantly buried from my feet to above my head in mere seconds.

The position I was frozen in was as if I were sitting in a chair. My legs were bent at a 90-degree angle; I never made it to the full crouched position. Both of my arms were also bent upwards at a 90-degree angle. My elbows were straight out in front of me and my forearms were completely straight upwards with my fingers stretched heavenward. My arms also never made it to the full shielded head position, but only made it upward towards the sky.

Because my head was buried into my chest and my arms were bent outwardly and horizontally near my head, my arms acted as a shield to my mouth and provided a tiny space where I could breathe and where, miraculously, no rocks had fallen. Since my head was bent downward when the rocks came tumbling down and filled in the area all around my arms and fingers instead, the rocks did not fill in the space where my mouth was. Though I was completely buried alive, from foot to head, God had provided an air pocket in which I could breathe.

I have no recollection of individual rocks hitting or injuring me, mainly because the landslide came as one massive fall. I was not struck by rock after rock, but simply submerged in one huge wave of rocks. I was still wearing my backpack and my full-body raincoat, which I am sure also shielded me from some of the impact of rocks on my back as well as preventing scrapes and scratches.

While I stood, or half-sat, in my frozen position, I was fully aware of the reality of my being buried alive. I was completely aware of my surroundings and could think clearly. I could feel the dampness of the cool wet earth around me and I could hear voices and movements about me. I was conscious that I only had a little air pocket and that I should not hyperventilate or go hysterical, or I would use up my oxygen. I was keenly alert that I must not breathe too deeply, so as not to hurt my lungs or back in any way.

As I sat, I began to listen. I knew Clive and Lawrence had been standing next to me when we heard the rumbling of the rocks. Yet, at this moment, as I listened, all I could hear next to me was a panicky mumbling and grunting noise. I wasn't sure if I was just hearing one or two people. The noise I heard was as if they wanted to speak, but their mouths were closed and no audible words could be spoken. It seemed that all that was left for them to do was to scream out, cry out through the use of sounds.

This grunting lasted for an excruciating minute and then suddenly I heard no more. I knew instinctively within my heart they did not have air and that rocks were all around their mouths. I knew medically speaking they had suffocated. There was no air for them to breathe and when there was no more noise, I realized they probably had lost consciousness. I knew then that they would die.

Then I began to think, "If I die also, how grievous it will be for my mom. For her to have her daughter die in a foreign country and to have to ship my body back to America would be truly awful for her."

Within my soul, I prayed sincerely that this would not be the case and, as I prayed, I received a genuine sense that this was not my time to go. I cannot explain that deep inner sense of peace within my heart and mind, but it was given to me miraculously by the grace of God. And because of it, I was somehow able to remain calm during this harrowing experience.

I then realized since I could breathe, I could also communicate and move my lips, so I started to call out for Josh to help me. When I cried out and he called back to me, "Where are you?" I was utterly relieved. He was still there and he could hear me! He told me he could not see anything but rocks and could not locate me though my voice sounded loud and clear. He sounded nervous, yet he seemed to also try to speak calmly and with strength in his voice. I had no idea what he could see or what he himself had just experienced.

He only later told me when the rock slide began to fall, he tried to run for cover towards that cement wall. But while he was in motion, the rocks fell so quickly that his feet and calves were instantly buried. He said that though his legs had been partially buried, he could lift himself out from under the rocks. While trying to do so, his shoes remained buried. He told me that nearly every person who was standing had been buried to some degree. Sam also was buried up to his waist and, only after he dug himself out with his own bare hands, was he able to escape and help others. Josh told me that though he had already unburied his legs, while trying to run again, a huge boulder fell straight on his back and pinned him down so he was completely unable to move. Sam used all his strength to lift that rock off him and then proceeded to unbury others he could find. Keiko had been partially buried. After moving hundreds of rocks away from her legs, Sam pulled her up and out of the rocks, but her shoes also remained buried. Sam and Keiko ran towards Shaowsy, who was buried up to her head. Because she had been wearing a large rimmed hat, they were able to locate her easily and they and the guide unburied her as fast as they could.

Meanwhile, Josh heard my voice calling out to him. Though the huge boulder had been removed from his back, he was still in incredible pain. He spoke to me as calmly as he could despite his own distress. He heard me, he said, yet when he looked up and across the twenty meters where we had all previously stood, he could see nothing but rocks in front of him.

I realized then I needed to do something in order for him to locate me. Since my fingers were up above my head, I thought I would try to move them to see if they could find the surface. Because the rocks had fallen downward at a 45-degree slope, they began to move and roll down the mountain as I wiggled my fingers. By the grace of God, the rocks were so placed that within only a couple of centimeters my fingertips were exposed.

I again cried out to Josh and asked him if this time he could see my fingers. I remember the first comment he said when he finally located me was, "You're all the way over there?" I did not know what that meant, but only later did I find out I was over ten meters from the cement wall. It was extremely painful for him to get to me since each time he crawled toward me, every move hurt his injured back. While I waited underground, after he had told me he located me, I suddenly heard him approaching me. It was as if being underground I could hear the hollowness of the rocks or ground above me.

As he came near, I could hear him beginning to unbury me. He seemed surprised that though he had found my fingers, he had not found my head. He started moving the rocks in a sweeping motion behind my hands and located my head. I felt him place his hands upon my head, and the mere touch of a human hand upon the top of my muddy, grimy hair was so exhilarating. He had found me!

~ ✢ ~

Josh located the top of my head and he started to clear the area in front of my face as fast as he could. He realized he had to move all the rocks which surrounded me at least one foot away so that they would not move back into the space which he had just dug out. Though I could not see anything, he told me that now he and Sam were together unburying my head. After several minutes, once my head was exposed, I tried to lift it up. The first thing I saw was the immense amount of rocks in front of me at a downward 45-degree angle.

All of a sudden, rocks began to fall again and though Josh was torn as to what to do, he and Sam had to flee for safety and scramble toward the wall. I could not see him at all since I still could not turn my neck, but unexpectedly, rocks started falling down rapidly all around me once again. This time, however, it was not one massive flow of rocks coming down at once, but individual rocks ranging from the size of a baseball to the size of a basketball. Then a rock hit me sharply on top of my now exposed head. I instantly saw stars in my mind's eye and my mouth tasted like blood. I was hit hard but miraculously I was not knocked unconscious. Adrenalin must have kicked in at this point because soon after that direct impact of the rock, I no longer thought about or felt the pain in my head. I only kept thinking about one thing: getting my entire body unburied.

I called out to Josh repeatedly over the next ten minutes and he tried to keep reassuring me that he would come back to me, but he needed to remain where he was until the rocks stopped falling. I remember waiting for him, being silent, but after some moments, I would call out to him again. I was unable mentally to just sit there and wait patiently; I really needed to talk to him and make sure he was indeed coming back.

During this time of waiting and not hearing any more rocks falling, I suddenly saw Sam running out before me.

Apparently when this second round of rocks started to fall, the guide had yelled out to everyone to run. Everyone but Sam and Josh ran off with him. However, after the rocks subsided, Sam got up from where he and Josh were crouching behind a cement wall, and went again to check up on Shaowsy. He tried desperately to get her attention, but she made no response. It seemed she was knocked out. He thought at that moment she had died, and he ran off after the others trailing behind them.

Since Josh was unable to understand Chinese and the command from the guide to run, and knowing that I was still buried, he waited by the wall until it was safe to come out. After a few minutes he told me he was coming. Once he arrived he tried with all of his might to remove the rocks first from my shoulders, arms and down to my back. It took a long time just for my arms to be freely exposed. Once they were, I tried with all my strength to also move the seemingly thousands of rocks which lay all around me. I first started to move those rocks from under my neck and push them with a sweeping motion away from me. Just to move the rocks from the area between my neck down to my stomach area took a long time and much effort. At one point I was so tired I just lay my arms down on the rocks to rest. When was I was ever going to be free?

While we were working around my torso and back area, I became aware of a sharp pain in my knee. I could not move my legs at all and, though it was as if I was just sitting on a chair, my legs felt frozen in a 90-degree angle. As the pain increased I kept reassuring myself that it was just like sitting in a chair so it should be okay. But my knee kept experiencing such a strange and awkward pain. I tried to ignore it and kept digging. It took about an hour before my back and upper body were finally exposed.

Because I was wearing my backpack, Josh had to dig all around it in order to free my arms. We wished we just had a knife to cut off the straps in order to release me so he would not have to exert so much effort to unbury my backpack. But without a blade, we continued to dig around the backpack and finally we were able to remove it from my back.

The freedom I felt to have half of my body exposed and freely moving was exhilarating. We were determined to finish the daunting task of digging me out completely so we kept at the slow and tedious job of moving each rock away from my legs. Once Josh was able to remove the rocks down to my knees, he stood in front of me and tried to stand me up. It was so freeing to be able to stand, yet because of the weight of rocks surrounding my calves and feet, I could not move. We had to keep digging. Soon after, Josh tried again to grab my arms and pull me out, but this only hurt my knee. We had to keep removing the rocks all the way down to my feet in order for me to be lifted out.

Once I was free, I tried to walk and make my way over to the cement wall, but I only limped. My knee was in excruciating pain and I could not put any weight on it. When we finally made it to the wall, we both collapsed there.

It was nearly 6:00 P.M. The rain was once again falling and darkness was fast approaching. I sat at the wall and kept thinking about one thing: While Josh had been unburying me, about ten feet away Shaowsy was still half-buried. I could hear her crying out at various times. At the time, I did not know who she was and did not find out till much later that she herself did not know anyone on this trip. Jesse, a friend of hers and an employee of SRAM, had invited her to go hiking with us. But Jesse never heard her alarm clock the morning of the hike and overslept. Though Shaowsy did not know anyone, she still decided to go hiking and now there she was partially buried.

Since she was in front of me when the avalanche fell, she was not completely buried from foot to head like the three of us behind her, but she was buried up to her head nevertheless. After Sam and Keiko had removed the rocks down to her waist, the second avalanche came crashing down. From that moment on, Shaowsy remained partially buried.

Josh and I pressed against the wall, clinging to it like rain-drenched vines, when suddenly Shaowsy started crying again. This time she cried out in broken English. Josh was barely able to hobble over to her in the darkness. He gave her some water to drink, yet quickly came back. He himself was exhausted, and though we both wanted to do something for her, we remained at the wall. I struggled all night with this decision. I had just read the night before in my Bible study with the Taiwanese in the gospel of John, "There is no greater love than this, than he who lays down his life for his friends." My heart and mind ached to help her in some way, yet I felt incapacitated. Though I was unburied, I now felt frozen and unable to move from the side of the wall I was sitting next to. Fear and terror had started to overcome me and though I desired to do something for this crying girl, I could not move. So all I did that night was pray. I specifically prayed for two things over and over again: For God to protect that girl, especially from any more falling rocks, and for the rain to stop. I was consumed with these prayers and I kept repeating them over and over with each hour that passed.

As darkness settled and the rain kept falling, I became immobilized sitting at the wall. I was afraid. The supernatural peace I had somehow experienced under the thousands of rocks during the hour and a half I was buried alive was fading fast. Now that I was able to move freely, I could not stop shaking. Terror was beginning to take root in me and not knowing how or if we would be rescued was gnawing deep within.

I kept asking Josh, over and over again. "What are we going to do? What's going to happen to us?" He kept telling me, "Terri, we are going to get off this mountain!" I wanted to believe him, but under the circumstances, I could not see how. Sometimes I would voice my thoughts out loud again to Josh and we would discuss whether there were helicopters available to rescue people like us stranded in perilous situations. Considering the weather conditions, could they even do this, I wondered? And would they do this since it would require grave risk and danger to them? Over and over again, we kept saying to each other, "Let's pray," and we did.

Josh and I soon became hungry and thirsty. We had been sitting at the wall for nearly an hour and we were cold and drenched from the rain. I started to shiver, not only from the cold night air, but also from the mounting fear arising in my heart. It seemed like every few minutes, rocks would come tumbling down the mountain, but we didn't know which direction they were coming from. Josh peered out from the place we were sitting at, and saw that there were some large backpacks near us, only a few feet away. He slowly and cautiously got up from the wall to see if he could move them near us. While he stood up, he again went quickly to check up on Shaowsy and gave her some water. He, like me, wanted to help her as best as he could. But due to his incredible back pain and it being pitch dark and rocks continuing to fall unexpectedly, he never ventured out for longer than a minute or two. He had the flashlight to lead him to her, but since it was only one narrow beam of light, and he could not see up the wide and vast mountain where the rocks were coming from, he always returned hastily.

When he came back, he proceeded to move the three or four backpacks he had seen nearer to us. On the outside of his own bag he had placed a sleeping mat which he could use under his sleeping bag. But instead, Josh took that mat and placed it over our heads. He put one side of it along the edge of the cement wall above our heads while we crouched underneath it. Then I remembered I had a hard boiled egg in my backpack as well as the apple we had received in the morning, so I got those out and placed the pack behind my back to lean upon. Josh found other fruit, granola bars and more water from the other packs. We ate and drank that which we found and again got ourselves nestled against the wall, cowering under the mat above our heads. I sat with my right shoulder pressed against the wall while I took the mat above my head and folded it up over my head and shoulders so as to shield myself from the rain. I bent my knees, though it was uncomfortable, as close as possible to my chest and Josh leaned back against them, though most of the time his weight was on my stronger knee. He also bent his knees in as far as possible so we both would have our entire bodies well guarded under the protection of our six-foot long wall.

Many times throughout the long hours of the night, the rain would start up again and come pouring down very rapidly and rocks would begin to fall at a tremendous force. Josh would ask me repeatedly to try to scoot back as far as possible, so he in turn could move back and have no part of his body exposed without the shield of the wall while more rocks fell. We sat crouched like that for hours, covered with the little mat above our heads.

Sometimes through the long hours of sitting and waiting, there was a glimmer of hope. One time we saw lights shining out beyond us, and we could hear voices in the distance. Josh stood up and aimed our flashlight towards those lights and cried out. We could see people on the other side making their way up the mountain from where the bus had been parked. At one point many of the lights merged together, but we realized they were still a long distance from us. They aimed their highly powerful beams onto the mountain area where Judy, Alan, Josh and others had crossed the smaller avalanche earlier. With the combination of their high beam lights and the lightning that was now illuminating the night sky and terrain all around us, we could see there was now a gigantic 200 meter long chasm separating us. The avalanche to the left of us did not seem to be nearly as active as this landslide area closest to the bus, but then again, that other one was now farther way from us and we simply could not hear it.

This avalanche, however, had grown wider, deeper, and absolutely impossible to cross. The chasm was at least 400 meters in depth and people later told us that huge boulders like the size of cars had fallen within this area. Thankfully neither Josh nor I had known when we had been sitting against the three-foot high and six-foot long cement wall, that just a hundred meters away from us that those rocks were causing such immense destruction. If I had known and seen what I was only hearing throughout the night, I would most certainly have been an absolute wreck. I was already becoming more and more terrified as the long hours slowly passed just with what I was hearing. It wasn't just like sounds of pebbles trickling down an embankment, but it was the sounds of continual crashing rocks and boulders after they had built up speed over a long distance of rolling downward, and plunging into other rocks. With every crash, I shuddered; I hated what I was hearing!

After maybe an hour, all of those lights which had shone directly across from us slowly, one by one, went back down the mountain until each of them disappeared and we were left all alone once again. The hope we had when we had first seen those lights had now evaporated and we were left by ourselves and to our prayers to God. It was truly heartbreaking and devastating to have been given such hope, only for it to fade off into utter darkness.

As we sat there in deathly silence, brooding over our future, Shaowsy began crying again. Since Josh had been standing up, looking out across the mountain as the last lights faded, he went over to her again to give her water once more and tried his best to reassure her. Each time he went to her though, he only stayed a minute because he was so terrified that at any moment huge rocks would come tumbling down and he would be caught in the midst of them. After he returned and sat down against the safety of the wall, Josh and I prayed together again for our rescue, for our protection, for Shaowsy, and for the rain to stop. Then we sat again silently, left to pray on our own.

After another long period of time, voices behind us called out to us. Josh tried to quickly get up and struggled to go as far past Shaowsy as he could towards the fallen avalanche where we had once crossed. Vincent was calling out to him from the other side. He yelled to Josh that a helicopter would not be able to come till 6 A.M. the next morning. It was nearly 11 P.M. at this point and the thought of huddling and waiting another seven or eight hours was an awful prospect. We not only were hungry, wet and cold, but the falling rocks were completely unpredictable. Josh yelled back, "No, we will not make it till then. We need to be rescued as soon as possible."

Who knew what the mountain had in store for us the rest of the night? Already a few big rocks had come so close to us and had literally flown over us and the wall, and even one of them had hit Josh in his upper leg. Though we were somewhat protected by the wall, it would not guarantee us no further harm, and Shaowsy was not safe at all. I just kept praying for her protection throughout the duration of the night.

Josh came back to me and reported what he and Vincent had yelled across to one another and we sat and prayed again. The rain beat down continuously over our heads, and not only could we hear the rocks tumbling down from the mountain, but the lightning and thunder that night seemed to be increasing in intensity. Because it was pitch dark, when the lightning would strike, it seemed as if the whole sky as well as our entire surroundings would light up. For a brief moment, if we peered out from under our little mat, we could see some of the destruction taking place all around us. The thunder which roared back in response to the lightning was deafening. And with the amount of rain that was pouring down and causing more of the mountain to give away with every passing hour, no wonder Josh yelled back to Vincent, "We need to be rescued tonight!"

After eight hours of constant torrential rain, falling rocks, perpetual lightning, crashing thunder and panic coursing deep within my soul, suddenly flashlights appeared just a few feet behind us. Evidently, some aboriginal people who lived in Ren Ai, a mountain village nearby, had heard of our condition from the TV and police. Within two or three hours after the avalanche, several of these aboriginal people had hiked down to where Vincent was located. They talked, discussed and debated for approximately four hours amongst themselves and with Vincent, whether or not they could rescue us. The risk was enormous and if they ventured out to save our lives, they would be putting their own lives in jeopardy.

As the time passed and they discovered that no helicopter could rescue us due to the rain and nightfall, they were also told that no police were able to rescue us either. After Vincent had talked with Josh, he finally turned to the aboriginals and said once again to them, "You are our only hope." However, at that moment the rain began pouring down again so they all ran further up the mountain to take cover.

The very place that the aboriginals and Vincent had been standing was now no longer safe either. When we all had first arrived at the site in the mid afternoon, we thought that place would be protected and secure since there were many trees above which could shelter us. But after severe rainfall and the avalanche area widening, large rocks started coming down through the forest above them, crashing and ripping the biggest of trees like chopsticks. One person reported that these rocks were flying over their heads at 100 kph or more, and one massive rock that landed on the trail they had once occupied and stood on, carried that section of the road down the cliff before their eyes.

Around ll:30 P.M. the rain started to subside a bit and, Vincent told me later, one strong aboriginal man by the name

Lee Ching Xiong suddenly grabbed a large rope and head lamp and literally ran into the darkness towards us. Two other men followed him who were apparently his relatives. Each one of them had to go over the same avalanche we had originally crossed, but now the risk was larger than ever. It was pitch dark, except for the sudden bursts of lightning which flashed out across the sky and mountain, and the stream of unexpected falling boulders would now become their greatest challenge!

Suddenly these three men appeared behind us. When they saw Shaowsy, they immediately began unburying her and had her out of the ground within ten to fifteen minutes. They hoisted her up on the back of one of the men and carried her towards the direction of the avalanche they had just crossed where Vincent was standing.

While they were helping Shaowsy, Josh got up to see what was happening. After they left, Josh came back, reported what they had done, and said they would return for us after they got Shaowsy to safety. But once we could no longer see them, just like the other rescuers who had shone their lights at us only to disappear from our sight, I was afraid they also wouldn't come back. Josh had not been able to converse with them in Chinese, but he reassured me that they would indeed return. Those minutes we waited for them seemed endless. I kept hoping and waiting, hoping and waiting, but panic started to come over me. I kept wanting to hope again, and believe they would come back for us, but I was also so scared that something might prevent them from returning. However, maybe after 15 or 20 minutes, they did return, just as Josh had said.

They immediately came to me and was I ever relieved to see them! I stood and tried to walk, but my knee hurt so much and I could not put any sort of pressure on it. One of the strong aboriginal men hoisted me on his back and I tried to hang on as best as I could.

When the man who was carrying me arrived at the avalanche area that we had crossed earlier that day, he stopped briefly and re-adjusted me before he firmly planted his feet and proceeded forward across the mountain. I was so scared at this point. I must have been shaking since I do not remember exactly how I did it, but I hit my arm on his headlight and knocked it out, which was our only source of light. He had to stop right there in the middle of the avalanche, hold me now with only one arm, and with his other arm turn his light back on. I was panic-stricken and I knew if he lost his footing, it would be horrific for both of us.

When we finally made it to the other side, Vincent was there to greet me. The man placed me on the road, the bank closest to the mountain, away from the cliff, and Vincent quickly came alongside of me. The first thing I said to him when I caught my breath and was sitting down was, "Clive and Lawrence are dead."

He said, "What?" And I repeated it again and told him they were completely buried. He cried out, "Oh no, not Clive!"

He also was aware that Clive was married and his wife was pregnant. But suddenly, Josh appeared with the other aboriginals and Vincent and I were no longer able to talk. The aboriginals and Vincent immediately began discussing what to do, and how to get us up to the mountain house.

Transporting us to the mountain house where we had eaten lunch earlier that day became our next goal. It was obvious, though I tried to take a few steps, I was not going to be able to walk. And the prospect of me being carried on the back of one of these men for two hours with my aching knee was not an option either. They began to consider their next plan and within fifteen minutes a motor bike came with a fairly large cart which was pulled behind. The cart was about the width of the road, five or six feet across and six feet long. Josh and I were instructed to be seated inside of it and they would drive us up the mountain road to the house.

I do not know what came over me at this particular moment, but I knew that I did not want to sit in that cart and be pulled by the motor bike. I knew the width of the road, and I remembered the various turns. If we flipped over, we would go flying over the edge and I could remember vividly my walk down with Bonnie and the drop-offs of 100-200 meters or more. The rain was pouring now and the thunder was roaring once again. With the lightning as bright as it was, I could see our path and its width all too clearly. The wheels of the cart were just on the edge of the mountain and I was terrorized to proceed.

I shuddered inside and asked Vincent again if there were not another way. Vincent assured me that this would be fine. I was battling within myself with every fiber of my being. This terrifying experience had taken its toll on me. The prospect of enduring another extremely scary situation was just too excruciating for me.

Within five minutes I cried out loudly, "I cannot do this. Stop the cart!"

Vincent must have realized how panicked I was and said to me firmly, "Terri, I will be right here. I will walk right behind this cart, right behind you the entire way. You will be okay."

I had no other option. I had to decide right then and there to trust his word, sit in that cart, and pray to God for this new situation. I placed myself as close as possible to the side of the cart which was next to the mountain and held on tightly. We moved forward and, just as Vincent had promised, he walked right behind us, as close as possible to the cart.

As I look back at this, the entire time up the dark and curvy mountain road, Vincent had to keep moving at a fairly fast and constant pace to keep up with the motorized vehicle. All the while, he was walking in the rain and traipsing through the mud, and this was after midnight. I can only imagine how exhausted he was, but he never once let on that he was tired. He only kept to his word and walked steadily behind us for the next two hours.

Several times along the way, while I was grasping the side of the cart, panic would grip me and I could not bear it. Fear would continue to mount up within me and escalate to a point where I just could not stand it. I had to have the cart halt and I would cry out again. Thankfully, the driver would stop the bike and, though it felt like everyone was wondering what was going on and why I stopped the cart, at that moment I did not care what others thought of me. Usually I absolutely hate to inconvenience others in any way. Yet when the fear would begin to escalate to an insurmountable point, I just could not help but stop the procession. Each time my question was always the same, "How much longer till we arrive?"

The first time I inquired, they said it would be about an hour. I shrieked inside; how was I going to last another hour on this precarious road? I would take a deep breath and Vincent and/or Josh would try to calm me down once more. I had to muster courage from within. I knew deep down that God was faithful and at those times I would try to remind myself, as Josh had told me so many times through the night, "We are going to make it, Terri. We are going to get off this mountain!"

Our journey went on what seemed like forever. Though they thought it would take up to an hour, it was closer to two. It was dangerous and precautions had to be taken. They were forced to drive slowly due to the rain and mud. All the while I sat clutching onto the side rail of the cart, looking up at the sky which was constantly being illuminated by the lightning.

Finally, after 2 A.M., we approached the lit up mountain cabin. I remember hobbling out of the cart and others immediately coming to my aid. As I came in, I was so glad to see each person. It felt like it had been so long since I had seen them. Actually, only ten hours had passed, but since each sequence of events was so dramatic in itself, it felt like an eternity.

When I saw David, the other foreign teacher at SRAM, I could not help but express how glad I was to see him. I instantly felt and said to him, "I am so glad you are okay." I was unbelievably grateful to see each and every person and know they were safe and dry.

After I made my way through the first and then second room where we had eaten lunch, I was ushered into a back bathroom where Jane and Bonnie came in to assist me. While everyone had been anxiously awaiting our return, yet not ever knowing when or if we would return, they had heated water for us and prepared large basins for us to wash in.

I was so weak and exhausted that I could barely hold myself upright on the toilet. Jane or Bonnie had to hold me up, while the other stripped me of each article of clothing. They finally got down to my skin and they rubbed a wet warm towel across my body. I remember the feeling of warmth was so pleasant but it lasted for only a moment since I was chilled to the bone. They put dry clothes on me they had gathered from others and escorted me to a back room to lie down. Though I had experienced the warmth of the water, I was still shaking and had to ask for three covers to be placed on me. I could not stop trembling from being cold, and probably from the fear, for hours.

For most of the night Bonnie sat down at my side though Darrin, Jane and Jack who are also employees at SRAM also came in to talk to me. While Bonnie kept trying to gather food, though we had meager and limited resources, Jack sat with me to keep me company.

Since I had been hit so hard on my head and had a huge gash on my scalp, they were afraid I would have a concussion and no one would let me sleep during the night. So while I talked with Jack, I shared with him about the incident on the mountain when I saw him trying to carry his daughter Kimmy across. I told him how I had prayed for them when I saw them about to cross the avalanche and the utter conviction I felt that they should not come to our side. I expressed the sincere heartfelt gratitude I felt towards God for preventing them from crossing. Though I didn't express it out loud, I thought and shuddered within myself that if he and Kimmy had indeed crossed, what would have become of both of them? I was deeply moved at God's protection over them and I could not help but convey this to him.

Jack continued to talk with me and, after Bonnie brought me some soup, he tried to help me to eat. He then shared his own beef jerky with me, though I did not know at the time it was the last of his own food. I was not aware of this until one year later when I was saying thanks to him again for his help that dreadful night. Once I heard the whole story from him, I went home that day and wept again. Even a year after that night, I could not help but cry all over again because so many had been so sacrificial and generous towards me on the mountain and over the months that followed!

Through the night, while in the cabin, when I was not talking with Jack or others who would come and go, Bonnie and I talked. She continually told me how glad she was to see me and how she had been so worried, how she had kept praying throughout the night, and how she had kept holding onto Jane's hand praying out loud everything she could express from her heart to God. She knew that Benson and Eric, both employees at SRAM and members of Banner church were praying for all of us also during the waiting hours.

Bonnie had witnessed the avalanche, and the enormity of its impact shook her deeply within her soul. She and those on the other side were staring in disbelief and shock, and she said at that moment, many desperate prayers were cried out loud by Vincent, Peter, Eric and herself. They stood there on the edge, crying out to God, waiting in silence to see who would emerge from the mounds of rubble. Bonnie said those moments passed slowly. After several minutes she saw only five of the ten people re-appear: the guide, Keiko, Lena, Arthur, and Sam. She could not help but wonder where the others and I were. She stood in silence, wondering and watching. Over the next few hours, most every one of the twenty-four made their way back to the mountain house where they tried their best to prepare food from their limited supplies, boil water and hold out with hope.

Not until one year later did Bonnie recount a story to me of that night. She told me that in the early hours of the night, while everyone was waiting for more news from those of us still on the mountainside, she went into the kitchen and saw four men, whom she believed to be Eric, Benson, Jack and Darwin, sitting there in pitch darkness and in utter silence. She said the grief, the sadness, the worry and the pain, though unspoken by anyone, was deeply evident and deeply felt. Even a full year later all she could say was, "The picture of those four men remains an unforgettable memory."

Back on the mountain, after the avalanche had subsided, the guide was trying to lead Keiko, Lena, Arthur, and Sam up and over the avalanche, safely back to the other side. But while they were walking, some huge boulders, the size of cars, were cascading down the mountain. The guide had climbed the farthest up, Lena was next, Keiko behind her and Arthur yet still further down. From what David, Vincent and Bonnie remembered, Keiko tried to cross over the avalanche directly. While crossing, she found a tree to hold onto, but was hit straight by one of those boulders and it landed on her, tossed her twenty meters into the air and down into the deep 300-400 foot ravine.

Bonnie and several others witnessed this though no one at that time knew exactly who it was since everyone climbing up the mountain was covered from head to foot in mud and silt. Vincent thought it was the guide and Bonnie thought it was a man also, but then the guide appeared shortly thereafter to all of them. They still did not know who exactly it was until much later, after a complete count of people was taken.

To this day, no one has ever seen Keiko again and her body has yet to be found.

As I lay in the base camp, shivering from the cold and fear, Bonnie told me about the person struck by the boulder, but still didn't know who the person was. Though I was listening to her tell me the story, I couldn't comprehend it. I heard the words she was communicating to me, but possibly due to my own shock and suffering, I simply couldn't make the connection that the person who had fallen was in fact one of the ten I had been standing with.

I then told Bonnie how I had been buried and how Josh unburied me and led me to the cement wall where we hid for cover throughout the night. I explained how terrible I felt for not helping Shaowsy, since she was also half buried. She kept trying to console me and told me we would all be okay, but I continued to feel so bad for not helping her directly. Thankfully Shaowsy was resting in the same room as me that night and Jane was carefully watching over her. She was unable to walk, but, thank God, she was alive and sipping soup like me. Josh had been placed in another room and was being tended by some others from our group. He also had been given warm water for his body, placed in a warm bed, and given some food.

Evidently, right after the twenty-four people on the other side of the avalanche saw the huge cascade of rocks fall, Vincent yelled out to everyone, "Whoever can pray, pray loudly and ask help from our Lord!" He also immediately called his wife Maggie again who was then working at Banner Church and asked her to pray and get help, too. He instructed her to call the Marines, the leaders of the military system who, besides the police, are also in charge of emergencies of Taiwan and see if they could do anything for us.

At the time of Vincent's call to his wife, around 4 P.M., Stephanie a teammate of mine and close friend, was also working in the same office as Maggie. When Maggie was talking to Vincent on the phone, Stephanie saw Maggie instantly collapse to her knees and start bawling. Another person on staff at the church took the phone from Maggie and continued the conversation with Vincent in order to find out the urgent details of the situation. Once the phone was hung up, the information was relayed to the others in the church office and everyone straightaway came together and began to cry out in prayer. Although Stephanie did not quite get the full scope of the story, she could tell that there was an emergency and that someone was in trouble. She joined the others in prayer, but it was not until Pastor Samuel's wife, May, came to put her arms around Stephanie to comfort her that she understood that Josh and I were involved somehow.

When I heard this story that everyone who was in the office began to earnestly pray and cry out to God for mercy,

I knew that all of their prayers on our behalf were what supernaturally carried me during the time I was buried. Even while Josh was unburying me, he had remarked a couple of times how calm I was. I knew then, after hearing Stephanie's description of the earnest prayers and travailing for God's help that was what had sustained me minute to minute during that horrific experience. The power of agreement in prayer is so great! I have known it before and seen its reality in the past, but having it demonstrated once again in such a significant and powerful way this time, continued to solidify its truth deep within my soul.

Stephanie told me later that though she had been a part of the earnest prayer at the church, she was still left with many questions about our situation on the mountain. In the stress of the moment, her Chinese coworkers were unable to translate the situation for her clearly or accurately. They themselves had only received a few pieces of information from Vincent and did not know enough to put the story together. Stephanie had wondered, "How serious is the danger? Are Terri, Josh, and Bonnie safe? What should I do now?" While she was thinking this, someone did reassure her that her three friends were probably safe in the cabin at this point, however, she said something in her spirit told her that was not the case. She immediately called some of the others on the team, Amanda, and my roommate Carrie, who were at work at the time, and passed on the scattered bits of information she knew and asked them to pray.

After work, Carrie, went home and started watching the TV for herself. Over the course of the night, various Taiwanese friends who were also watching the news called her and conveyed what the reports were saying. Carrie called Stephanie back to tell what she had been hearing and seeing. The news started saying that there were three people dead, some people buried, and some partially buried on the mountain.

As the evening continued, Stephanie also received updates from Linda, a staff member at Banner who oversaw all of us foreigners. Each time Linda called, she painted a clearer picture of the seriousness of our state on the mountain that Thursday night.

The first update told them that three people had been buried alive and that I was one of them.

Thirty minutes later they were told that Josh had dug me out and that my knee was hurt.

The final report said that a helicopter could not pick us up until 6:00 A.M.

After the first update, Stephanie contacted everyone on our team to explain our situation and to ask for prayer. One teammate, Elliot, was over at Stephanie and Amanda's house that night when they received the first call from Linda. He immediately tried calling the police to see if he could gather any further information about "the hikers on Tun Yuan Mountain." Alarm really broke out within our team as the messages were passed on to everyone. Many of the members gathered at Stephanie's apartment to pray and comfort one another. Several members decided to stay up interceding for us until the early hours of the morning.

As morning approached at the base camp and the fog began to lift, we learned a helicopter was going to approach at a nearby site and Shaowsy and I were going to be lifted out and transported to a hospital. Though I had calmed down somewhat during the night, I did not feel I had the strength to endure another scary endeavor. I pleaded with Bonnie for another way off the mountain. But it seemed there was no other way.

Around 7:00 A.M., though it was still very cloudy outside, the rain had stopped and the fog had lifted. It appeared safe for the helicopter to approach the mountain house. Suddenly I heard a commotion going on and I was told I needed to get ready to leave right away. I had desperately wanted Shaowsy to be taken off the mountain first, but I was told she needed a stretcher and the helicopter had not brought one. Therefore, I was next. Josh would follow after me and Shaowsy would come later. I put some other pants on, and begged Bonnie to come with me and take my backpack.

Someone, whom I did not know at the time but now know to be one of the aboriginal people, carried me out to the helicopter site. As I was approaching, I was distraught again. The helicopter was hovering over an open area and two men from up within had hooked up a big cable which was attached to a metal basket. They lowered it down and I was carried over and placed inside the basket. I started shaking all over again. How long would it take to hoist the basket up to the helicopter and how long would I be left dangling, flying in mid air? I really didn't want to do this, but I had no choice.

I was buckled in and the men who had helped me get into the basket told the men up in the copter to reel me in. Slowly and gradually I moved upward as the basket swayed to and fro. As I approached the door of the helicopter, the two men grabbed the basket and bolted it on and securely fastened it. I was moved inside and left sitting on the floor. They lowered the basket again and moved forward with the same procedures and brought Bonnie up to me. Was I glad to see her!

Once she came in and was sitting next to me on the floor, it took off, flying down over many of Taiwan's majestic mountains. Because the fog had lifted, I could see the vast expanse of ranges. We were far up in the mountains and it took nearly thirty minutes to fly to our destination. Someone must have told them I was a Christian because they could have flown somewhere closer, but instead they flew me to a Christian hospital in Puli.

Because my teammates Stephanie and Amanda had been informed the night before we would be helicoptered off the mountain, they waited anxiously for any further news. Around 7:00 A.M. Friday morning Amanda and Stephanie got the call from the church saying that we were being helicoptered to a hospital and asked if they would like to ride in the van being sent to meet us there. After hearing this good news, Amanda called Carrie my roommate, who quickly gathered some belongings of mine, while Stephanie and Amanda went to Josh's apartment to do the same for him. Carrie called her school and took the day off to come and see me in the hospital.

On the way to Puli, Stephanie had received a phone call from her mother, Susan. Thursday night, Stephanie had sent an emergency prayer e-mail once she understood our situation better. Though Susan had not yet read the e-mail, she told Stephanie that God had already put me on her heart and that she had been praying for me fervently in the U.S. without even knowing what had occurred. After updating her by phone, the girls went to a 7-11, grabbed some food that they knew we would like to eat and drove in the van for the two-hour trek to the hospital to meet us in Puli.

As the helicopter neared Puli, we landed on the large track and field area of a high school. After they dropped me off, the helicopter took off once again to the mountain to bring down Josh and another SRAM employee, Arthur, whose leg was injured. An ambulance was waiting for me and I was put on a stretcher and driven to the hospital, alongside of Bonnie, while the sirens noisily blazed through the city streets. Bonnie and I were immediately transported to the emergency door, and I was ushered to a ward with about six beds. The curtains were closed around me and soon a doctor approached and began speaking to me in English. He asked where I was hurt and I told him about my knee. He decided to do an x-ray of it, but while we were talking, he said I should get a tetanus shot to prevent any disease. I couldn't understand. What kind of disease could I have contracted since I was just buried under mud? I hate needles and I hate shots. But, again Bonnie encouraged me and coaxed me to be safe. I reluctantly agreed and took the shot.

The doctor then asked me about my head. I told him a rock had hit it, but mostly the pain I was experiencing was in my knee. I did not realize that blood was mixed in with mud all over my hair. They tried to separate the hair from my scalp, and they took a picture of my scalp where the rock had hit and showed it to me. I was in complete shock. There was about an eight centimeter gash on my scalp. It did indeed look like a bloody mess, but because twelve hours had already passed since the impact, the wound was dry and appeared to me to be sealing itself. The doctor told me I needed to get it stitched up. I did not want to get stitches in my head! Though the wound looked horrible, it did look dry. But he explained to me it could reopen. I asked if I could have some time to think about it.

As I lay on the bed, I desperately cried out to God for an answer. Did I in fact need these stitches or not? As I prayed and waited, I felt in my spirit it was not necessary. I asked God again and felt for the second time the same way. Over the years I have prayed like this and have grown accustomed to what I feel is the Holy Spirit giving discernment.

Bonnie had been talking with the doctor and giving him information about my experience. When she approached me, I told her what I had felt impressed with during prayer. She was extremely disappointed and felt I absolutely needed to get stitches. She told me it was a huge gash and it could not be left unattended. I asked her if she would also pray. I explained how I prayed and tried to discern the difference between God's will and my own. So she prayed, but came back and told me she did in fact feel I needed to get these stitches. I was stumped! Was my will so resolutely opposed to getting these stitches that I only heard what I wanted to hear? I was seriously confused at this time.

Little did I know at the time, but this sort of confusion would plague me over the upcoming days and weeks. Praying and seeking God's will, normally a pleasure, was to become a true challenge for me. Something about the experience on the mountain seemed to have rattled, or even severed, my ability to hear God clearly and vibrantly. This struggle over the stitches was a minor, initial example of a greater problem to come.

Usually I am a team player and like to work alongside people. Even if I do not agree or see eye to eye on something with them, I do not like to move forward until we all agree. I do believe God can speak to both parties who are seeking His will and give the same answer. And yet here Bonnie and I were not sensing the same direction. Though I felt it was not necessary to get stitches, I could also see how distraught Bonnie was if I didn't get them. I thought about all she had done for me. I did not want to break any unity with her and I wanted nothing to separate us. Though reluctant, I made the decision to go through with the procedure since she felt so strongly I needed to get it done, and asked her to stand alongside of me when I got it sewn up.

But before I was to be stitched up, we were escorted to the x-ray room to examine my knee and head. We then went back to my original area and shortly thereafter Josh arrived next to me. He had just been helicoptered down and had talked with the same doctor and told him about his back. Evidently, he also had been hit by a rock on the head and was instructed to get stitches. He readily complied. I told him how I was told I also needed to get stitches, but how I did not think stitches were necessary in my case. After he looked at my head, he said my gash was much more serious than his and I did indeed need them! I was very scared, but both the doctor and Josh told me it would not be bad. In fact, Josh volunteered to get his done first and during the sewing, I halfway looked on while they did it. The thread was long and I watched them go up and down through the skin several times. Josh re-assured me again, it was not that awful. I knew I was next and I had to do it.

Bonnie came and stood by me while they shaved off the hair in that area to clean it before they began stitching. They first shot me with a numbing agent, but frankly it was too weak. I could still feel the needle going in and through my scalp. I winced and held tightly onto Bonnie's hand while they proceeded to put eight stitches into my head.

When it was finished, the doctor came back and told me that he had viewed my x-rays and no bones were broken. I asked why there was so much pain, and he told me that probably the inflammation around the ligaments was causing the severe pain. There was really nothing they could do as far as rehabilitation went until the swelling went down.

The last problem I needed to talk to the doctor about before I left was my fingernail. Then, with all due respect, I showed the doctor my middle finger. It had been hit by a rock; it was now black and blue and the nail was filled with blood. The doctor told me it needed to be drained and he proceeded to take out another needle to insert it into my nail. I complied, reluctantly again, and winced at the pain while he drained it. After that, medically speaking, he said I was ready to go.

Moments later, I heard English voices and when I looked up from my bed, there were my teammates Stephanie, Amanda, and Carrie, my roommate. They hugged me and expressed their sincere gratitude for my well being. I did not know what came over me, if it was their expression of love or the simple fact that I was with friends again, but I was overcome with tears. Amazingly enough, not once through the entire ordeal of being buried, trembling with utter terror during the dark hours of the night, making it across the mountain on that rickety motorbike cart, or making it safely to the hospital in the helicopter, had I ever once cried. Yet, seeing their faces now and feeling their love overcame me; I could not help but sob. It was wonderful to see them and they were equally as happy to see me and Josh.

Within minutes, Linda also came over and briefly talked with me, feeling so relieved to see me. Linda had taken such good care of us foreigners over the last couple of years while we were living in Taiwan and it was good to see her.

When the doctor finally released me to go, Linda and the other girls got me prepped to leave. Stephanie warned me that many cameramen were outside waiting for us to be released. I was shocked. I certainly was in no mood to talk to anyone. Bonnie, on Vincent's behalf, and Linda encouraged both Josh and me not to share anything with the media. SRAM wanted only one official representative from the company to be the spokesperson.

I also did not want to be seen on camera. We decided Stephanie would be a decoy and attract the attention of the camera men while I would be wheeled out by Carrie and Amanda. I decided at the last minute to put a jacket over my face so I would not be seen. I did not want to talk and I did not want to be hassled with a barrage of questions by anyone, so I thought if I covered my face, they would not ask. Never did I think though that they would broadcast us live on TV, even with my jacket over my head. But they did. And they also broadcast Carrie saying to them, "We do not want to talk right now; we just want to get her home."

But when we arrived at the van and I was moved from the wheelchair to the vehicle, I needed to see what I was doing. So while I briefly removed my jacket, the camera men did catch my face on film. Thankfully they asked no questions.

As we drove in the van over the next couple of hours back to Taichung, I told the girls about the avalanche. They had heard some of the story through the various phone calls, but as stories go, many details were unclear and vague.

As I began relaying the story to the girls, I felt again the enormity of it all. After two hours of driving, as we entered Taichung, the girls suggested we stop to get some sandwiches so we could all eat together at home. Stephanie and I stayed in the van while the others went to get our lunch. I had been sitting up during the ride, but now I decided to lie down on my back.

As I gazed upwards toward the ceiling of the van, I no longer noticed the metal or scratches engraved into the ceiling, and I began to fade away quickly into thoughts about Lawrence and Clive. Here I was alive, breathing, brought back to safety and soon approaching home. But they were still in the mountain, buried alive, and now presumably dead.

I could not contain my emotions and I began to feel sickened, grieved, overwhelmed, and at a loss of understanding. Since Stephanie and I were alone in the van, I felt free to just speak all the questions of my heart out loud. Why had this happened? Why did God not stop the rain? Why did we go on this trip when the weather was not good? What would have happened to me if Josh had not been there? Why was I still so afraid? Where was God in all of this? Could I ever close my eyes again and not picture all of this? What was my life going to be like now? Stephanie tells me she prayed for me during this time, but I don't even remember it.

The other girls came back with our lunches and climbed into the van. I could not control the anguish deep within my soul. Why was I alive? Why were they dead? I could not comprehend it and I began to sob with a sick heart. Amanda immediately began praying for me and I could feel the warmth of her heart. I needed prayers and I needed someone to pray for me. Though my heart was so heavy-laden with pain, her words brought God's love and comfort.

Next, Stephanie sang out a long song about suffering, yet trusting in God. I had not heard the song, but I tried to concentrate and join in prayer with her words. It had been good for me to sob; I needed to have that freedom and release in my soul. Looking back, I truly believe that initial weeping was a start in healing for me. I needed it to be released and it needed to be expressed.

Finally we made it up to my apartment, and I sat in the living room with the girls and tried to eat my lunch. It all felt so strange—being home, finally off that mountain, having survived, and now eating lunch as usual. It was almost incomprehensible. We watched the news to see what they were saying about the avalanche. We saw some of the images of the mountain and we even saw the footage of us when we were leaving the hospital. After all of this, I was getting tired. I had had very little sleep in the past 36 hours and I felt I needed some time alone with God. I asked the girls to assist me to bed. Amanda readily helped me to go to the bathroom, and she set towels on my pillow since my hair was still a muddy mess. I had pleaded with the nurses to wash my hair in the hospital and, though they had indeed put my hair in warm water and tried to shampoo it some, it was still a long way from being clean.

I will never forget my reaction when I was finally left in my room alone lying on my bed. My entire body was aching from limb to limb and the mere movement of trying to roll from my back to my stomach took an immense amount of effort that my body did not have. I lay there in excruciating pain. I knew the impact and pressure of all those rocks was finally taking its toll on me. Though no one could see any scratches on me, since I'd been covered by many layers of clothing, the pressure of rocks all over my body was now felt internally.

This discrepancy — between my visible, external wounds and my unseen, interior wounds — would become a major struggle for me. My spiritual condition over the next several months would follow the same pattern my body had felt in the course of one day: while I may have appeared okay on the outside, I was injured and immobilized within. I had come off the mountain safely, yes, but over the coming weeks I would feel a series of delayed reactions to the avalanche at the spiritual level. Just as I lay on my bed taking stock of my body's internal trauma, so over the next few weeks I would discover wounds deep within that made even the simplest spiritual efforts feel exhausting. My usual energy had been squeezed out by the avalanche's paralyzing, unseen damage to my bones and muscles. Likewise, my usual "lightness" with the Lord would be replaced by a heaviness of soul that drained me, though I knew not why.

I remember that when I was buried, I could not move anything except for my lungs and finger tips. The mere movement of my lungs, in a slow upward and downward motion, took such effort and felt so strained. Now, here I was able to move my entire body, but it took extreme effort from every muscle. I finally made it onto my stomach to rest. Shortly thereafter, I heard my door open, but I was unable to look up to see who was there. Evidently, Cherry, my good Taiwanese friend who had previously worked for SRAM, had watched the news and knew from the TV that I was going home. She had been glued to the TV most of the night and waiting, trembling with suspense, for the latest updates. As soon as she could, she drove down from the north of Taiwan, and came to my house to see me. It was just after 4:00 P.M., and when she entered, I tried so hard to lift my head from the pillow and turn it towards her.

She was crying and was so glad to see me. I also began to cry again and told her how sad I was over the loss of Lawrence and Clive. She just listened and let me speak. After some time, I knew I could not lie there any longer. I was uncomfortable and knew it would be better for me to get up and move into the living room with the others.

The girls ordered pizza that evening and we sat down to eat in front of the TV. Josh's back was in considerable pain, and he just laid there flat on our living room floor on his stomach with his head propped upward in order to eat. He had been driven home in a separate car and came straight to our home where Carrie and the girls could take care of both of us together. Many of our team members called asking if they could come by and see us, but we replied that we were only ready to see a few people. So only Kathy and Heidi, a couple other girls from our western team of teachers, came over to us that night and spent time with us. The others from the team decided to come by the next night, Sunday, to show their support and pray together.

When the news would come on TV about our experience, we would all become quiet so Cherry could translate it for us. We saw pictures of the team of twenty-four trying to maneuver their way off the mountain another way. They had to cross an enormous river with the aid of a pulley contraption. I looked at the TV screen and saw Sam's face as he squatted on one side of the river while someone was being carried across by the pulley. I could not help but wonder what Sam was feeling and experiencing during that long excruciating day and at that exact moment. My heart really went out to him and the others. I could only hope and pray for their well-being, for them to get off the mountain safely and come home soon.

Eventually, I was exhausted and had to go to bed. Amanda and Cherry helped me as best as they could and, after the door was closed and I was on the bed with the light turned off, I again felt so strange. Only 24 hours before I had been on the side of the mountain's cliff, trembling in fear, and chilled to the bone from the cold and rain. Now here I was in a warm apartment and on a soft, comfortable bed. Time no longer seemed to fit together. Past, present, then, now, here, there — it was all jumbled. I felt like I had emotional jet lag. My body was in my room, safe and warm, but my soul was still trapped in many ways on the mountain, wet and terrified. I was unburied in the present yet still buried in the past. How could such a series of dramatic events happen in such a short time frame? It felt like each hour in and of itself had been an entire day's event.

I tried to think clearly, but was only left in confusion and without a perspective of time. I lay there in bed for a long, long time, going over every situation in my mind and trembling over each sequence of events. As I relived each moment and every emotion, I began to get more and more frightened. The emotions of fear were mounting within my heart and I felt like I couldn't control them.

I suddenly cried out, yelling out into the darkness. I could not stand it. I was so scared with each and every little noise that came from either the outside or from within our apartment complex. While I had been waiting on the mountain, I had heard hundreds of rocks fall with such force throughout the night so that now any sudden noise startled me and sent a chill down my entire body.

When Carrie heard me cry out in panic, she ran over to my room and quickly opened my bedroom door, turned on the light and asked how I was. I told her I was scared and I needed prayer. For as long as I can remember, whenever I was scared or needed God's comfort, I would pray and talk to Him. His precious Word in the Bible says that we can cast all our cares on Him, for He cares for us, and I truly believe this about His character. I have seen and I have experienced Jesus' compassion towards our cries and because He hears our every prayer, I told Carrie I needed and wanted prayer.

Carrie quickly phoned over to the girls' apartment and since Amanda and Stephanie lived just across the street from us, they were over within minutes. They all sat down with me on my bed and began praying with me. They prayed that Jesus, our Mighty Savior and Deliverer, would take away all fear and the terror of the night before which now plagued my soul and mind. They had heard my story in the van on the way home and knew I had been traumatized. They asked for God's peace and asked for Him to comfort me.

As each one of them prayed aloud, while I had my eyes closed, I truly agreed with each of their prayers and lifted up my heart and soul into the Presence of Jesus. After about 30 minutes, after each one of them had prayed for me, I felt much more peaceful. Since it was already 2:00 A.M., they left shortly thereafter. It was good to pray with them and I was so grateful they came and I felt their love, compassion and care for me yet again.

I drifted off to sleep soon after and slept well into the morning. From that night forward till this present day, I have never again experienced a fear or terror of loud noises due to that dreadful night on the mountain. From the moment the girls and I prayed together, I have not had one nightmare, nor any form of a panic attack due to a jolting noise.

Nothing.

I have heard loud sounds at night, and thunder has roared powerfully against my window panes, yet even through the dreadful typhoon season of Taiwan, I have never been terrified again of loud noises. I simply experienced a miracle through those initial times of prayer and they were critical and crucial for my inner emotional healing of fear of loud noises. God was merciful to me and completely answered all of our heartfelt cries that night and came to my rescue when we came together in prayer.

PART II: Revived

"Healing of the Body"

Physical Recovery

The next morning, on Saturday, though I was still weak, I did have a little more strength. The night's sleep had done me well and as Carrie and Cherry prepared breakfast for Josh and me, Carrie's cell phone suddenly rang.

"Hello, Terri?" my mother said.

"Yes, this is Carrie," answered Carrie.

"Terri, this is your mother," replied my mother.

Carrie kept saying, "This is my mom? Mom? *My* mom?"

"Terri?" my mother asked.

"Mom?" Carrie answered. "*Mom?*" The experience had all of us more than a little confused.

After a few minutes, Carrie figured out that it was in fact *my* mother and our team organization's leader had given my mother Carrie's phone number instead of mine.

"Cherry," said Carrie, "this is for Terri."

Carrie passed the phone to me and I was surprised and even shocked to find my mom already knew of my condition. Evidently when Stephanie had sent out that emergency prayer email, she sent it to the director and he contacted my mother. Thankfully when he called her, he prefaced to her first that I was okay and at home safely, but there had been an accident.

We talked for nearly 45 minutes that first time and I tried as best as I could, to tell her the story, yet reassure her that I was alright. Little did I know at the time, but just having installed SKYPE on my computer only three months prior, I would be talking with all of my family and closest friends regularly. I did not know the emotional and psychological trauma I would experience and the absolute need to talk with my family and loved ones. They in each of their own way, would become a type of counselor as they gave me their listening ears and helped me to process the trauma.

After breakfast and the talk with my mom, Cherry drove Josh and me to a hospital near our house. Josh was in a lot of pain and evidently, the doctor from the hospital in Puli had called that morning saying that he looked at Josh's x-rays again, and there was indeed a hairline crack and he needed a back brace. The doctor had already told us the day before that we needed to get the stitches in our head sterilized daily for the next five days so we needed to find a hospital we could go to in Taichung. Now the doctor was informing Josh that he needed to get a back brace, too.

I also wanted to see a doctor who was close by our home and ask what further treatment I needed for my knee, as well as get my head looked at, so off we went to the hospital. When Cherry arrived at the hospital's entrance, Carrie jumped out and got a wheelchair for me. Since I had arrived home, I hadn't done much walking at all though Carrie had loaned me crutches she had from a previous accident she had had. Sitting in the wheelchair felt awkward, but the reality was I could never have walked throughout that hospital on crutches while we looked for the various departments we needed to contact.

After Cherry parked the car, she and Carrie helped Josh and me in and through the hospital for our further examinations. We found the place we needed and, as we were sitting in the waiting hall to see the doctor, the person across the aisle from us was reading a newspaper. It caught our attention. Our picture was displayed on that page!

The day before, while Josh was in the hospital sitting down getting ready for his x-ray, and when I was getting into the van, we were photographed. We were both shocked and Josh and I immediately began talking to each other. Cherry and Carrie joined in our surprise. The four of us must have been staring, because when that person reading the newspaper turned the page and saw our photograph in the newspaper and then us in front of her live, she seemed to not believe her eyes either. She kept looking back and forth, up at us, down at the newspaper, up at us and back down at the newspaper to see if in fact who was before her eyes were really the same people photographed in the newspaper. We never did talk with her, but we knew we needed to get a newspaper for ourselves. We hadn't ever talked with any reporters about anything so we were curious as to hear what they were actually reporting.

After Josh and I visited with the doctor, got the back brace and had our stitches sterilized, we arrived back home from the hospital fairly early Saturday afternoon. We sat in the living room, with the TV on, watching the news since it kept reporting bits and pieces about our hiking tragedy. Soon after, many visitors started to come one by one.

Most visitors in the first couple days were from SRAM but who had not been on the hike with us. They had been either back at the office working steadily trying to help in whatever way possible, or keeping abreast with the latest updates. Jason came over for awhile, as well as George, both English students of mine at SRAM, yet when Elbert came, we probably talked the longest. He had been in Colorado, working at SRAM's Development Center when he heard the news and was anxious to get back here to Taiwan to assist in any way. He told me he had been nervous and wanted to know personally how I was. He brought me chocolates, wrote a nice note to me, and like Jason and George and the many other SRAM employees who came in the following weeks, Eric, Harry, Stanley and Jeffrey, he expressed his heartfelt care and concern.

The next day, Sunday, we again had several visitors. We all sat in the living room watching the news. Our friends had brought the newspapers for us and translated the content for us. In the following week, it seemed that nearly every newspaper in Taichung covered the story about the hiking accident. They included in the coverage pictures of our last group photo together, beautiful pictures of Keiko, Lawrence, and Clive on his wedding day with his wife, as well as Josh and me. Sometimes the story would take up an entire page. Over the weekend, the newspaper described how the other twenty-four had to hike out of the mountain another way. Since they had been stuck up at the cabin that first night and there was no direct road off the mountain through a designated trail, expert hiking guides from Taipei and all over Taiwan were asked to assist the group the next morning. Several of them volunteered their services and escorted them down what turned out to be an incredibly grueling and dangerous hike.

A year later Jack told me that while he was hiking with the guides, he or others would keep asking, "When will we arrive at the bottom?"

The guide would continually reply with the same answer, "I do not know when we will arrive. All I know is the direction we need to go and we need to just keep moving in that way."

Jack said he had wanted some reassurance, but he, as well as the others, never got the answers they wanted. They simply had to keep walking and trusting they would eventually reach their destination. Jack told me they were all exhausted from the trauma and lack of sleep the night before, but they had to hike off that mountain, with little time for rest or reflection.

In the beginning, the entire group of twenty-four tried to stay together. Jack's ten-year-old daughter Kimmy, stayed with him in the front of the pack. But after some time, when the entire group had congregated at a well known waterfall, the guides decided they had to divide into two groups in order to allow those hiking without lights to get off the mountain before sunset.

Six men went with one guide and the other fourteen, including women and children, were assisted by several other guides. Since Jack was in the first group, he had to place his daughter into the care of one of the guides in the second group. Jack told me though they had already experienced many strenuous and difficult hours of hiking, his daughter never cried. Yet, when he placed his daughter's hands into the guide's, Kimmy began to cry, telling how afraid she was that they would never see each other again. For Jack it was an excruciating moment.

By this time the group had no more water, was completely exhausted, and running low on optimism. Nevertheless, they had to move on and part ways with the other group. The men in the first group gave all their head lights to the second group and were told their aim was to make it off the mountain before nightfall. Jack said it was urgent that they hurry. And as the guide led, each person had to follow right in his foot steps so as to not get separated from each other even for a moment. At one point, Jack said, his eyes drifted away from the person in front of him, only for an instant, and he suddenly realized he wasn't with the group. Thankfully though, he caught sight of the group again through the brush and quickly ran to catch them. They simply had to keep moving forward and keep persevering. They did not know where they were. They did not know how far they had left to go. It was still wet and getting darker. There were no trails and they not only had to bushwhack over several areas of growth, but sometimes had to cross over huge boulders without any rope assistance.

One time they came to a rough and flooded river, which the guide told them they had to cross since they had to head that direction. As soon as Jack stepped into the river, the water rushed up to his calves and nearly swept him downstream, so powerful was the current. The guide realized that in order to get everyone across, he needed to stand in the middle of the rushing river, brace himself, and take each person's hands to assist them across. Jack couldn't see any road or path on the other side of the river. Only huge rocks lay before his eyes. The guide kept urging them to approach the rocks. When Jack came close enough, he saw that it had a five-centimeter edge to it. The guide told them that they had to place their feet on it, stretch their arms vertically up and over any rocks they could hold on to, and traverse the wall upward, away from the river. They hiked like this for over a hundred meters until they found wider and larger boulders to climb on. Unfortunately, while Jack was crossing up and over one of the many huge boulders, he lost his footing and nearly fell to the rocks ten meters below. He mustered the little strength he had at that moment and climbed up as hard as he could to the top. He was so scared, and worried not only about himself, but also constantly about his sister and daughter. If he was barely making it over this rough road, through the river and over the boulders, what was happening to them? How could they make it? "It was very, very tough," Jack said. "I thought I would never see them again."

Thankfully, within only two hours after they had separated from the other group, they finally found the hiking trail that they had been searching for. As they neared the end of this long-sought path, there was a large rushing river before them. Fortunately there was already a wire pulley across the river and several other people had gathered there to assist them across. Meanwhile, news reporters stood by hoping to catch it all on film.

Each person, individually, had to be carried across by a wire pulley. When I saw this footage on TV that weekend, my heart nearly broke. David, the other English teacher from Canada, looked absolutely exhausted when he was being pulled over to safety. I noticed the anguish and pain in Sam's face as he waited for his turn on the other side of the river. Sam later told me that hike down was horrible and during those grueling 24 hours, all he wanted was to *get off that mountain.* He had seen firsthand the mighty hand of God in nature. Though he was not yet a believer in Jesus at that time, through the traumatic events of the hike, and then through reading the Bible for weeks after the hike, he came to recognize God's power and love. (Ultimately, not long after this period of trauma and spiritual reflection, Sam placed his trust in the Lord).

Finally, near nightfall everyone had made it across to safety. The group of fourteen was only 15 minutes behind, and the women and children were once again reunited with the men after many hours of their own excruciating trek on the tangled, off-beaten roads. All twenty-four of them sat down on the bus in near-total silence while they were driven back to Taichung late Friday night.

~ + ~

We were so appreciative of the many visits of guests from SRAM, and especially when they told us that the other twenty-four were safely off the mountain and all at home. I was so relieved and grateful each one had made it down. I knew, like me, they needed lots of rest since our bodies had been stressed and shocked from everything we had been through and it had taken its toll on us. We had eaten little while up on the mountain, and our bodies needed to be nourished and replenished after all that we had gone through.

Thankfully, also, during those first couple of weeks, when I had so many guests, the food was nonstop. It seemed that whoever came brought food and we always had more than enough. I believe with all my heart, the food that we ate those initial few weeks, was truly beneficial to the health and healing of my body. With each passing day, with a rich source of vitamins and iron, my body seemed to literally soak it in.

One of the greatest blessings that first week after the accident was a lady, Surrina, from my Friday night Taiwanese Bible study. Evidently, an offering had been taken concerning us and she in turn, took that money to buy food for us and came over several times to make us a three or four course meal. The first meal she made for us was first class steak and we were touched deeply by her generosity, cheerful and loving heart, and her ability to cook such outstanding meals. Every meal she cooked, as well as every dish that was brought over to us by others, was always prepared not only for Josh and me, but also for Carrie. The love and care, generosity and kindness expressed daily were overwhelming. Not only was I receiving fabulous food for lunch and dinner, but Carrie made me breakfast every day for nearly two weeks since I was unable to carry food at the same time while walking with crutches.

On Sunday night, most everyone from our English teacher's team visited, along with a few of the staff from Banner church, Stephen and Sabina, and Linda. Again, not only did several of them bring us fruits and cakes, but that night they all gathered around to pray for us. Specific prayers were uplifted on our behalf and not only for our physical healing, but for our emotions and mind. I remember being touched by the people who were praying for us, and yet, deep down within my own heart and soul, I felt numb.

Something deep within me still felt I was stuck up in the mountain. Yes, I had been touched deeply by the prayers the girls had previously prayed for me when I was terrified of the noises at night, and God had truly answered those heartfelt cries. Yet, this time, my mind and heart didn't seem to calm down. I couldn't stop thinking about Keiko, Lawrence and Clive.

I wanted to receive the prayers of all those praying for my inner emotional state, but it was as if I could only hear the words of their prayers, since my heart was unable to grasp it. I wanted to feel and understand their prayers, but everything seemed so strange to me.

Even though I was there in body in that room, trying to receive their heartfelt prayers, it was as if I couldn't remove myself from the trauma and experience of the mountain. Every emotion I had felt in those 18 hours up on the mountain, whether it was fear, or terror, or uncertainty, I had felt with every fiber in my being. Every scene I saw, the rocks all around me, the flashes of lightning revealing the destruction taking place, Shaowsy half way buried, now all flooded my mind. I had gone through too many intense and excruciating emotions and coping with survival moment by moment took every bit of energy and effort. Granted it was approximately only 18 hours in total, but every hour, and literally every minute, consumed my soul, mind, heart and emotions. Every minute I was thinking, "What is going to happen next? Are we going to survive? How are we going to get rescued?"

And now, there I was, safe in my apartment, with life seemingly as normal as the days before I had left for the hiking trip, but I couldn't seem to comprehend any of it. I felt completely disoriented. The prayers people were speaking were heard by God and they were beautiful and precious, I'm sure of that, but I was unable to have them touch my heart. I wanted them to permeate my heart, but I felt distanced from them. Therefore, I just tried to receive their prayers and after they finished, I genuinely thanked them for coming over.

I went to bed that night knowing Monday was going to be another intense day because I had been told by someone in SRAM, there was going to be a press conference with SRAM and the families of those who had died. Nothing had actually been discussed with the reporters or media yet. At the time I didn't really know what this press conference was going to entail, but I knew I would be relaying the message of the calamities on the mountain.

The next morning, after a good night of sleep, Carrie was serving me breakfast, and again various people from SRAM came over to bring us lunch, and also to drive me up to the office. When I first arrived, they carried me into the nearest downstairs classroom and it was there that I met some of the ladies from the office, Aileen, Melissa and Joanne. I began speaking about the avalanche and briefly told them how we had all been standing and how Clive, Lawrence and I had been completely buried alive. I told the ladies how I heard Clive and Lawrence, struggling and trying to gasp for air, and how after a minute or so, there were no more noises; only silence.

Suddenly, Judy came in and I hadn't seen her since before the avalanche when she had asked me to go down with her to the bus those brief moments together. I warmly greeted her and we were both so moved to see each other. She then told me we needed to go since we were going to tell the reporters about the accident. I told her I would tell the story as honestly and precisely as I could and share the details of the avalanche and Lawrence and Clive's deaths.

She suddenly exclaimed, "We need to hold out with hope that they're still alive."

I was so taken back by her words that I was left speechless and I just stared at her. Does she not know they are dead? Does she really believe that are still alive? Is this a type of coping mechanism to think or hope they're still alive?

I was so stunned at her comment, and with the fact that I had just shared with the ladies about their death there in the classroom minutes before she came in, I couldn't help but say to her, "Judy, they're dead. We all were completely buried alive and they had no air. I heard them trying to gasp for air, but they had none. They're not alive."

But she replied back to me, "Terri, we need to hope. To hope they're still alive!"

I was still left speechless but I asked her if she had heard the story yet and it seemed she hadn't yet heard all of it. I then asked her if she would be translating for me for the press conference since her English was really the best, and she said, "Yes."

After she said that, a deep heaviness settled over my heart. I felt and sensed it would be difficult for her to hear the full scope of the story for the first time, and then translate it all at the same time. I knew then this press conference was going to be a hard and tough task to do for all of us.

Again, someone from the SRAM office, picked me up, placed me in one of their cars, and drove us down the street to the China Trust Hotel where the press conference would be held in one of their conference rooms. I sat down and briefly met with F.K., the Vice President of SRAM who had flown in from Chicago, SRAM's headquarters. He told me he would be conducting this meeting and wanted me to share about my experience. Soon after talking with him, Judy came, picked me up on her back, climbed up the stairs and carried me in the conference room.

I was astonished! There were so many people and many reporters with huge cameras and several video cameras. There must have been at least 8-10 reporters, plus another 30 people in the conference room. I found out later that most of those people were the direct family members of Keiko, Lawrence and Clive, as well as the three guides who led us on this hike, various SRAM employees and all the managers of SRAM.

F.K. began the meeting by stating that the purpose of this time was to share with the families as accurately as possible about the events which led up to the avalanche. The main speakers were the guides, Vincent, F.K. and myself. Not everything was translated for me, but I did recognize the guides and Judy briefly translated for me how the guides said they had received permission from the national park to hike, they had indeed checked the weather and were told there was not to be a storm. They had been hiking guides for years and they bragged and shared how SRAM's company worked well with their own planning and organizing of the trip. They obviously were not amateurs, nor was SRAM ignorant at all in the arena of hiking and planning trips such as these. They all shared with as much convincing proof that all such precautions had been made prior to the trip.

I was one of the last to speak and I must have spoken for at least 20 minutes with translation. I stated first that I wanted to tell the story as accurately and precisely as I could with every detail possible. I began telling the story from beginning to end until I finished with being rescued by the aboriginal people. As I looked out at the faces around me, I tried as best as I could to look them in the eye and communicate my heart. I wanted them to know the sincerity of my words and the truth as best I could explain.

F.K. then opened up the meeting for discussion and questions and many of the family members asked several questions pertaining to the weather, the specific hiking trail that was chosen, and then finally, the compensation for their losses. Many questions and answers went back and forth for approximately 45 minutes. It was an intense time of discussion and it was obvious the families were trying their best to assess and understand what had happened on the mountain. Emotions were raw and, though I didn't get everything translated, I could see on the various family member's faces, the dissatisfaction with the answers that were being given. They were obviously still in shock and grief, and anger was mixed together throughout their expressed words, tones and looks on their faces. It was a very hard and sad encounter to watch and be part of.

After some more discussion, F.K. made some concluding remarks and the meeting was over. I remained seated where I was, and ended up having two distinct conversations at great length with Clive's sister, as well as, Lawrence's girlfriend. Both of them could speak English fairly well so I did my best to try and explain the details and situation to them again. Though they had heard me speak and share, they wanted to understand the situation more. Little did I know it would be the first and last time I would ever talk with them and I am so thankful I had that opportunity to share in the press conference, as well as, talk to them face to face more intimately and personally. I really felt their losses and my heart truly ached with theirs. When I spoke with them, I couldn't help but look deep into their eyes and try to communicate my love, care and concern for them. I wanted to comfort them; I wanted to hug them. I wanted to talk and share for as long as they wanted and needed.

And so we did, but then it was over after nearly 45 minutes, and Judy once again, carried me down the stairs on her back and someone from SRAM drove me home. I remember sitting in the car, so sad and so full of deep emotions again. This was all so hard and painful. I kept asking myself, "Who am I and why am I the one allowed to live? Why must I be the one to share about the loss of their son, their brother, or boyfriend?" My heart was hurting so deeply!

I went home exhausted, spent of emotions and could barely communicate or engage in any sort of conversation that night. I went to bed early.

~ ✦ ~

The next day, on Tuesday, I was again called up to SRAM to meet with F.K. and the Taiwan SRAM leader Hank Gowe and others. They wanted to know if I could draw a picture or try and describe the exact location where Clive and Lawrence were buried. Since Vincent and some of the others had already gone with a high powered camera and taken pictures of the exact site of the avalanche, they wanted to show these to me and ask where they should start digging. They had captured pictures close to the cement wall where Josh and I had huddled for hours. I tried as best I could with descriptions, drawings and measurements from the wall, to explain where I believed Lawrence and Clive were buried. They told me because there was such a massive amount of rocks which had fallen and had continued to fall over the course of the past three days, it made the digging a difficult and tedious job.

Lawrence and Clive were not unburied until exactly seven days after the avalanche. I prayed daily they would be found. Every day I asked someone from SRAM if they had found them and each day they said no. On Wednesday night I had a specific dream that they were found and unburied. It was so real and so precise in my dream, I truly felt and believed when I awoke, that Thursday would be the day they would be found. I talked with Judy briefly on the phone that morning, and asked again if they had been found and she said no. I told her I believed they would be found very soon.

Samuel and Joanne would come down every afternoon to bring me lunch and bring me to the hospital. I still needed my stitches cleaned every day. I asked Samuel that day if Clive and Lawrence had been found and he said he believed not. However, around 2:00 P.M., while driving in the car to the hospital, Samuel received a call that they had been located and were being unburied. I literally started to cry. I told Samuel how I had had a vivid dream the night before and had been praying for them to be found and was so grateful.

The next day when I saw Samuel, he told me that their bodies had been unburied and brought to a morgue for their families to identify them. I was told later by Lawrence's mom that when they identified him, though he had been buried for seven days, his body was still quite well preserved. They believed that since the mud was still wet, cold and damp underground, it acted to preserve his body, and his family said he really looked fairly well. This was a small relief for them in an otherwise horrific ordeal.

Though already one week had passed since the accident and I was being so well taken care of by many of the employees of SRAM and the members of Banner Church through the constant supply of food and drives to the hospital, my heart and emotions were still a mess and wreaking havoc on me. My heart still felt like I was bound under a ton of rocks, continually feeling the effects of the smothering darkness around me. I had written a two-and-a-half page description of the accident to all of my family and friends within a few days after my rescue, and though I had received so many heart-warming and beautiful emails from them, my heart was still feeling unresponsive to it all.

Many dear friends wrote encouraging Bible passages from the Psalms for me to read. Psalm 46:1-3 says,

> God is our refuge and strength, an ever present help in trouble. Therefore we will not fear, though the earth give way and the mountains fall into the heart of the sea, though its waters roar and foam and the mountains quake with their surging.

One would think after reading that verse, I could completely identify with it since the earth had indeed given way and the mountains had fallen, and God certainly had been my refuge and strength. But after reading it, though I tried to meditate on it and understand it, I just couldn't grasp its meaning.

Psalm 40:1-4a says,

I waited patiently for the Lord; he turned to me and heard my cry. He lifted me out of the mud and mire; he set my feet on a rock and gave me a firm place to stand. He put a new song in my mouth, a hymn of praise to our God.

God had indeed lifted me out of the mud and mire. So while I read this verse, why couldn't I see this or comprehend these words of truth?

Psalm 91, a favorite of mine says in verses 1-7, 15 and 16,

He who dwells in the shelter of the Most High will rest in the shadow of the Almighty. I will say of the LORD, 'He is my refuge and my fortress, my God, in whom I trust.' Surely he will save you from the fowler's snare and from the deadly pestilence. He will cover you with his feathers, and under his wings you will find refuge; his faithfulness will be your shield and rampart. You will not fear the terror of night, nor the arrow that flies by day, nor the pestilence that stalks in the darkness, nor the plague that destroys at midday. He will call upon me, and I will answer him; I will be with him in trouble, I will deliver him and honor him. With long life will I satisfy him and show him my salvation."

This entire psalm speaks of God's protection, how He is our refuge and how we do not need to fear anything, yet again I was having a hard time grasping it.

One last verse that had been given to me was Psalm 23:4-6 where it says,

Even though I walk through the valley of the shadow of death, I will fear no evil, for you are with me; your rod and your staff, they comfort me. Surely goodness and love will follow me all the days of my life, and I will dwell in the house of the Lord forever.

Though I had my Bible by my side when I lay on my bed or when I sat at the computer reading people's letters, when I tried to read the words, focus and concentrate on the meaning of each of them, I simply could not. It was as if there was a blockage on and over my heart. I felt bound within, deafened to the words of God by the rumbling of falling rocks. Though I knew I desperately needed God's healing words to touch my soul, the words simply remained words of ink on white paper rather than penetrating my heart like they had usually done in the past when I read God's precious Word.

In my life, though I had been through my own set of trials, pain and deep suffering, never had I felt so empty and void from God's words in the Bible. Only two years prior, when I was going through some of the most excruciating pain of a broken relationship and friendship, the death of my beloved grandmother and the selling of her place which I called home, I always felt God's precious Words as my source of strength and comfort. His Word was my bedrock which held me firmly and solidly to Himself.

However, this time through this trial, though I tried to read His Word from the Bible, and especially those precious verses people had given me, I felt removed from them. This sorrow of pain and time of questioning left me so weak. I couldn't stop grieving in my soul, and my head was in a constant array of thoughts thinking about Keiko, Lawrence and Clive's lives being lost and mine still being granted to me. I tried to function as best I could: I tried to eat, I tried to engage in conversations, but always I asked, I wondered, I pondered, I questioned, "Why am I here and the others dead?"

My sister works for an ambulance company that provides emergency 911 services in Northern California. In one of the first talks over the computer with her, she told me I was probably experiencing what is known as "Post Traumatic Stress Disorder" (PTSD). PTSD occurs after a trauma or life-threatening event when someone has difficulty being in touch with their feelings, or being able to express emotions. It's as if they are emotionally numb and the person will feel detached, have trouble concentrating, or is unable to stop thinking about what happened.

I was not only suffering from the trauma of all I had encountered with the avalanche and being buried alive, I was also struggling with what she termed "Survivor's Guilt," a feeling of immense guilt for being alive while others died. She said that after a critical crisis, one needs to do what is called "Critical Incident Stress Debriefing," which typically means doing therapy or talking with a counselor to recover. SRAM told us they were going to hire a counselor for all of us, but it wasn't going to start until another week due to many other logistical things needing to happen first. My sister told me it's vital to start debriefing and counseling within the first 72 hours after the trauma. However, just having the time to talk with her, plus my brother and his family the previous day for over an hour, as well as my mom, was very beneficial.

I also began talking with my dearest friends back in California, Bob and Ruth, who acted like adopted parents to me. They, as well as my mom, were invaluable to me during the countless hours of talks we ended up having over the computer phone. I felt after each one of our talks and the honesty in which I shared about my pain, was helpful for me. I didn't hold back anything of what I was feeling, or thinking, or questioning, but I voiced it all to them. Looking back, those talks became invaluable to me, and in the end became a big source of healing and a type of counseling for me. I needed their love, their prayers, and their listening ears, sometimes for a full hour, and they always gave it to me warmly.

~ ✦ ~

Samuel and Joanne, employees from SRAM, became my soul caretakers. Evidently, the SRAM management divided amongst themselves and the employees which people and jobs needed to be attended to over the course of the next several months. Samuel and Joanne were given the "task" of providing for my needs and taking care of me. They provided my meals, since I was unable to go out to restaurants or for groceries the first few weeks due to having to walk with crutches and keep up with daily hospital visits. They truly became what I affectionately termed "my angels". They are both such loving and kind people and we enjoyed each other's company. They became two of my dearest friends.

During my many hospital visits, though the x-ray had shown no broken bones, the swelling and pain was so great in my knee. I kept feeling like I needed to get an MRI. I felt I needed to say something or do something about it but I didn't know how. The first weekend I was home, because the newspapers and TV news were reporting this tragedy night and day, my Chinese teacher Sophie found out about it. She immediately tried to contact me and on Sunday she and her husband, Ming Li, a doctor at China Medical Hospital, visited me. He did a careful examination of my knee and head and gave me some pain killers and anti-inflammatories.

I voiced my desire for an MRI, so right then and there, he called the hospital, but told me there was a waiting list up to two weeks. I was devastated. I wanted to proceed immediately with treatment for my knee and start a physical therapy program.

The next day, however, I was delighted to see Chinese culture work in my favor. Thanks to what the Chinese call *guanxi* — which literally means, "relationships" but really means, "It's all about *who* you know" — I was able to get an MRI scheduled for the following Wednesday by one of Dr. Li's good friends.

On Wednesday, the day of my MRI scan, as well as the following day when I received the detailed report from Dr. Li's friend, a knee specialist, both Joanne and Samuel assisted me. They were there to help translate for both the doctor and myself. The MRI results revealed I had no torn ligaments, but only severe soft tissue damage called, "bone contusion" which ended up being a large bruise on the side of my femur bone where evidently rocks had been pressed. Also, a large amount of fluid had gathered under my knee cap, causing the swelling and discomfort. The doctor spoke with me for nearly 20 minutes and said he believed that within two weeks the fluid would most likely dissipate and after a few months of physical therapy, my knee should be back to normal. He re-assured me it would be fine and wanted to start me on therapy only at the end of the following week, to allow for some extra time for the swelling to go down.

The following Thursday, I had my first physical therapy appointment and it was astounding how crowded the exercise room was. There must have been between 20-30 people working out in a fairly small two-room facility. The P.T. assigned to me was very caring and attentive, when time permitted, but he was a busy man and obviously overworked. My treatment lasted two hours and the drive to the hospital was at least 30 minutes from my home. In total it took three hours to complete one P.T. program. The following day it was the same procedure and I was concerned about Samuel and Joanne missing so many hours of work since they themselves had projects and dead-lines to keep. I kept thinking over and over in my mind what to do. Again, God in His great mercy provided a solution.

Over that weekend, my dear friend Maggie, who was also an employee of SRAM and former student of mine, came back to Taiwan from a six month stint in America. Her first night home, she and Jane, the one who had bathed me and helped take care of me at the mountain house, came over with dinner. Maggie told me her main project for work was finished and she had more time now so she could help me out. We decided to see if we could switch hospitals to one closer to my home and do my physical therapy there. We wanted to try it out the following Monday and I deeply thanked God in every way. Not only was the drive less than 10 minutes away, but the P.T. office was staffed with at least three to four physical therapists. It was not crowded so they were able to give me undivided attention for an entire hour.

The first day I was there was certainly the most painful. After a massage of my knee, I was asked to lay on my stomach. My knee was bent at a 90-degree angle while buried and though two weeks had passed, it was still unable to straighten out. The physical therapist wanted to take my calf and foot and try to manipulate and stretch my leg downward so it would eventually lie flat down, instead of sticking straight up to the ceiling. She pulled and pulled it downward and I yelled in pain and began to cry; it hurt terribly.

At that point, due to the stiffness and lack of movement, I wondered if it would ever be stretched out and normally lie flat again. Maggie took me back nearly every day that week and by Friday, only five days later, my leg had been stretched downward to an approximate 120-degree angle. I was relieved and knew then I just needed to be patient throughout this entire healing process. It wasn't going to happen quickly and I needed time, as time itself does do its beautiful work over the course of weeks and months. I had to be patient and endure, and continue to trust in Jesus throughout this entire process.

PART III: Restored

"Inner Healing of the Soul"

A Resurrection

Before I started my physical therapy, while I was waiting for the swelling under my knee cap to go down, I slowly made my way around to various places. Since Josh and I were unable to go to church the first Sunday we got home off the mountain, we went the following week. A lady from church came to pick us up right outside our apartment complex and drove us to church. Thankfully, we arrived a little early so we didn't make such a commotion with our awkward entrance on crutches and our need for a special seating arrangement.

Since Josh's back was still in pain and he needed to lean against some pillows and I needed pillows under my knee, Stephanie and Amanda arranged for two big couches to be placed at the back of the sanctuary for us to sit on. Some church members came over to greet us, but for the most part, since we were in the far back, I didn't feel too much attention was focused on us. This was good for me because again, though I was there in body, my heart and mind were still experiencing the numbness and lack of emotion and feeling.

The songs were being displayed on the screen one at a time during worship and though I tried to comprehend their words and meaning, I couldn't grasp or internalize them. It was as if I was just mouthing the words, reading them, but unable to sing or experience them in my heart.

Finally, as we began to sing the last song for the morning, we sang a new one that I didn't remember ever singing before. The words began with, *"When troubles come, I trust in You. For I know you will lead me through. And I know You are faithful till the end."*

I could tell with the start of these words, this particular song was moving me. The words continued, *"And when the storms are drawing near, when I'm with you, I don't have to fear. You're my Shepherd on whom I can depend. Through the day, through the night, I know You're always by my side."*

By the time the congregation was singing these words, I started to cry, but when we got to the chorus, I started to sob.

*"Lord you are always here with me. There is no changing,
God, in Thee. You are the same yesterday and today and forev-
ermore. Here on your promises I stand, you hold my future in
your hand, my solid rock, almighty God, I worship You."*
Every word in this song resonated within my heart.
These words I could relate to. These words I could understand. These words began to soften deep places in my mind
and soul.

After two weeks of feeling bewildered and disillusioned
about having been spared the throes of death, I felt I was
finally emerging from the darkness into the light. I was stepping out of my emotional prison, and I felt an exhilaration at
that moment as strong as when Josh had unburied my head.
At that time, I rejoiced to have at least that much of my body
unearthed. I could see and hear and breathe deeply again,
though I was still unable to move the rest of my body. There
was still so much to be unburied, and I was still vulnerable
and weak, but freedom was in sight.

So, while this song was as liberating for my heart as
Josh's hands had been for my head, I knew it was only the
beginning. Yet breathing the air of freedom once more, I
could indeed hold my head high and sing out loud, *"When
storms are drawing near, through the night, I know You're
always by my side."* I began to weep since I knew afresh
God was with me and He did hold my future in His hand.

Since it was the last song to be sung and Pastor Samuel
must have been asking, as he did in every service, if anyone
needed prayer to go forward. I must have not heard anything
since I was now lost in my own heartfelt sobs for one of the
first times since the accident. Yet suddenly, many people
gathered around me, and around Josh, to pray for us. I was
crying and I was hurting and though I couldn't truly catch or
understand all the prayers at that moment, I do believe that
was a significant time of healing. My heart had been softened,
moved and opened to the Spirit of God. Many dear brothers

and sisters in the Lord gathered around me, agreeing in prayer for my healing. After it was finished, I was at a loss for words to express my feelings and emotions.

Pastor Samuel then walked all the way from the podium to the back of the sanctuary with a microphone to have us share briefly, which I had agreed to do earlier that morning. But when the microphone was given to me, though I spoke for a couple of minutes about the avalanche and my rescue, I honestly don't remember exactly what I said. It felt as if I were just mumbling.

Pastor Samuel, as well as some others, placed their hands on us, in accordance with the Bible verse in James 5:14-15,

> Is any one of you sick? He should call the elders of the church to pray over him in the name of the Lord. And the prayer offered in faith will make the sick person well; the Lord will raise him up.

He prayed for a few minutes for both of our healing in the name of Jesus Christ. After he said, "Amen," he walked back to the front podium and resumed to give his sermon.

I can't say I remember much about the sermon that day, but I was touched that Pastor Samuel and others had prayed for us and our healing, and I was especially touched that when I sang that song, I was able to experience God's presence and love in a newer way than in days past.

After the service, many people came up to us and expressed their heartfelt gratitude to God to see us alive. I had already seen many of them Friday night since I had invited all of those from my Taiwanese Bible study of John to my house. It was good to see many of them that night, and now to see so many of them again on Sunday, as well as several other members from the church who were my friends. It warmed my heart and I was glad to receive their hugs and see their tearful, yet, joyful eyes at our presence. It was good to feel their love and I needed to receive it. After we talked with various people, we were taken home and again, Stephanie, Amanda and Linda joined us for lunch and fellowship and it was a sweet afternoon.

The following day, Monday, was another outing for me and probably one of the most difficult days I had during that first month. Lawrence's family was at a funeral parlor and friends and relatives were allowed to visit, talk to them and pay their condolences. Jeffrey, one of SRAM's leaders, and Judy picked me up and drove me over to a Buddhist temple area near Lawrence's home where Lawrence's mom was sitting, grieving.

When we first entered, the first thing I saw before my eyes was a large hanging photo approximately 36 inches by 24 inches of Lawrence. My heart was pierced to the core. It was so sad to see his beautiful shining face and dark brown eyes lit up in the photo, and know he was no longer with us. Flowers were everywhere, in order to honor him and show respect to the deceased. Incense was also being burned for him in front of his photo. I was told later that incense is burned to create a comfortable atmosphere for him to go peacefully. Pineapples, cakes and various other foods had also been placed in front of his photo, in order to provide safe travel to his next destination, where he would find a new dwelling place. The food is meant to strengthen him to arrive in the next world, which some Taiwanese call the "West world," a peaceful and joyful world. All of these rituals emphasize and reinforce the Buddhist tradition that the deceased's family will take care of him, honor him and provide for him in his new life.

We sat down on the benches and waited for his mom to finish talking with three young adults, who were obviously Lawrence's friends. When she finally came over to sit and talk with us, I was by this time choked up and at a loss for words. Here was her beloved son, dead, and me, a foreigner, buried alive right next to him, but alive.

I was overwhelmed by the emotions flooding over me. There I was, sitting in this Buddhist temple, with only fans blowing on us during a hot humid day, facing the mother of one of my own deceased students, and I was unable to speak. I felt sick to my stomach and I nearly wanted to throw up. I knew I needed to remain there seated besides her and do the best that I could to talk with her. She had told Jeffrey she wanted me to come so she could talk to me, and I had wanted with all of my heart, to meet with her, also. Yet, at that moment, it took every ounce of prayer within me, to cry out to God for His beloved mercy and grace.

What words of comfort could I give this dear mother?

She began asking me to again retell the events leading up to the avalanche. I told her about all of us crossing over the first mud slide area, and how after the wood plank had been laid, Josh and Lawrence wrapped the rope around their waists so as to assist the others across in order not to fall.

I shared about our last talk while we watched Josh and Alan cross safely down to the bus and how we also wanted to be assisted down when Josh returned, but how the rocks began falling once again at a more rapid pace.

I told her about our calls to the police and how when we had heard the loud rumbling and roar of the mountains above us, Clive, Lawrence and I had people on either side of us preventing us from moving anywhere and we were forced just to back up our bodies against the mountain's face.

I told her how we were instantly buried from foot to head within seconds and all I could hear after the rocks subsided from falling, were the grunts and moans of what I believed to be Lawrence and Clive trying to gasp for air.

I tried to explain as best and as gently as I could, that I sincerely believed they did not have any air pocket when they were buried. I tried to convey that with the sounds they were making, it was as if they had rocks up and around all over their mouths and nostrils. And because the grunting noises subsided and completely stopped after only a minute or at most, two, I believed they lost oxygen, and therefore, lost consciousness. This was an agonizing moment for me. I was trying to share what I felt were the facts, since I was the only person there on the mountain with her son and could tell the story to her, but it was extremely painful to be so blunt and real. And yet, I continued on and told her that after it was silent, it was as if I knew inside my gut, they had lost oxygen, had passed out, and were going to die without that source of oxygen.

She then asked me, why, after I was unburied, didn't we at least try to unbury them? This was definitely one of the hardest and most agonizing of questions. She had hoped that they could have been spared and still be alive.

I again tried as best as I could to tell her, it took over one and a half hour to unbury me and when it was finished, it was nearly nightfall. And though we were clearly able to see Shaowsy, we didn't have what it took to unbury her, let alone try to unbury two people we could not see. We ourselves were extremely weak, in considerable pain, and the rocks were continuing to fall. These moments of discussion were the most excruciating, painful and dreadful for me. I felt utterly sick inside, trying to communicate what I believed happened to them and all I could do was cry out and pray silently to God during that hour of talking with her.

The conversation shifted and she told me that when they had found Lawrence's body it was well preserved. But she then told me an interesting fact.

When the rescuers found Clive and Lawrence, their positions were unlike mine; they had put their entire upper torso flat down with their heads face-down into the mud. When I heard this, though I didn't say anything out loud, I knew then my instinct had been correct. If they had placed their bodies toward the ground, and with that amount of weight, and the force of rocks that fell upon us so quickly, it would have only pushed them both that much harder into the ground. No air pocket would be possible and they would have no oxygen. Again, talking with Shaowsy, a week later, she also confirmed that when she turned back to look up at the mountain right before the rocks fell, that out of the corner of her eyes she saw them both put their torsos face down.

When there was nothing more to say to Lawrence's mom, except to express my deepest apologies and sympathy, we got in the car to drive home. But within only a few minutes, I asked Jeffrey to stop the car. I felt sick and I couldn't sit in a moving car. I didn't know if I would throw up, but I had to have the car stop. I began to cry and I moaned how hard and difficult that conversation was for me.

Jeffrey then said to me, "Terri, we won't have you do that again. You don't need to talk about it anymore with anyone else."

He had heard everything and knew how horrible it was for me to revisit those memories, to try explaining them one more time. And yet, though I welcomed his sympathy, and though re-stirring the emotional waters was devastating for me, I felt I needed to talk with this family and do my utmost to share with them. Yes, I needed a break for a while; but I didn't want to say, "No, I never want to speak or share about it with them again." I knew they needed to hear, to listen and to try to understand, and I knew at that moment, I had to do it for their sake. I also knew that just as God had provided the strength and grace to make it through the conversation with Lawrence's mother, He would prove faithful to give the strength and grace for future conversations. Assured of His provision, I resolved then and there, no matter how difficult it was to share, I would not shut them out.

And so I went home absolutely wiped out. I lay on my bed for a long, long time, thinking, mourning, and grieving.

~ + ~

The next day, Tuesday was our first day of Group counseling at SRAM and again, Samuel and Joanne brought me lunch and drove me up to the office to meet with the counselors and with those from SRAM who could attend. Though there were thirty-eight people on the hike, only eighteen people were direct employees of SRAM. The others who had attended the hike were either spouses or relatives, children, or friends of the employees.

Of the eighteen employees to attend the first counseling session, only eight people who went on the hike attended. This disappointed me because not only is my Bachelor of Arts in Psychology, and I believe strongly in counseling, I knew for all of our inner healing, it would be most beneficial if all of us were there, just as my sister had said. I sat down with the other eight, hoping others would come later and Maggie sat by my side translating for me.

It was then that I heard the first hand account of their stories. Most of them in the room that day were people on the other side of the avalanche and most of them saw Keiko hit by the massive boulder and fall off the cliff. They were truly struggling with what they saw and many shared their pain and internal struggles of the memories within their mind.

It was then that I heard Sam speak for the first time since I saw him running off before my eyes when I was buried. He shared briefly how the guide had called them all to run up the mountain and cross to the other side. He hadn't seen Keiko fall, but he, like all of us, was very scared and frightened for his life.

I also shared my story with the others as best as I could. It was probably the first time that they heard from me, as it also was my first time hearing from them. I think it was beneficial being together, but unfortunately, the second week during our scheduled counseling session, only three people showed up and, after that week, no more people came. I don't know why it never worked out to do these counseling sessions, since there were probably not too many other places or people to talk with and through this tragedy. And it seemed beneficial to have a place and time where people could freely talk. But since it did not continue at SRAM, I ended up talking nearly every day with my mom and/or Bob and Ruth. Their listening ears, caring hearts and prayers were vital for me and processing with them through the entire situation helped tremendously.

Two weeks after the accident, on Saturday afternoon while Carrie, my roommate, was out, I was left alone for several hours for nearly the first time since the accident. No visitors came by. Cherry hadn't been able to come down that weekend, and I had the apartment to myself. I tried to write some emails to various friends, but after some time, I was overcome with the sadness of the situation again. It was as if every fiber in my being wanted to cry out, but I didn't know how.

I lay on my bed again. I don't know if I did exactly cry out to God for help or if He just knew my heart's desire for comfort and strength, but that afternoon, both Vincent, and then Judy, called me just to see how I was doing. It was one thing trying to talk to people who were not there about the accident, but entirely another thing to talk to people who were there. They, in many ways, experienced and understood the situation. I'm sure both Vincent and Judy, as managers of SRAM, felt the weight and pain and loss as much as anyone else, if not more.

I talked freely and openly with them and they both encouraged me in the Lord, since, thankfully, both of them are Christians. I felt touched and uplifted by them, and after hanging up the phone, I softly cried with gratitude because I knew that is what I needed, and God the Father had provided their words of encouragement and comfort for me.

Even so, I was perplexed by my situation. I had begun physical therapy, my stitches had been removed successfully from my head, and I was being taken care of tremendously everyday by SRAM employees and friends. Yet, my emotional and spiritual state remained unchanged, even despite the Banner church service that had touched me so much. At that hour in the service I had felt free, unburied, for the first time since the accident. I had breathed the fresh air of God's Spirit.

But within a day, the wind was knocked out of me again. It was similar to the elation I had felt when my head was first unburied — only to be struck suddenly by a tumbling rock. The spiritual freedom I had felt at Banner was also shattered by a sudden blow the very next day, a blow as surprising and disorienting as that rock had been to my exposed head. After church on Sunday over the next few days I continued to try to read the Bible, but my heart and mind could not focus on anything else but the trauma and tragedy. I constantly found my thoughts drifting back up to the mountain, remembering Keiko, Lawrence and Clive. I was grieving, and though I didn't know it at the time, I was in need of an outlet for the emotions bottled up inside. I didn't know how to release them because I didn't know how to get in touch with them. Blow after blow of grief and guilt tumbled down on me, leaving my soul spinning. It was as if I was thinking about everything every moment, and yet, feeling numb towards life all at the same time.

As the weeks passed, I was still unable to read or concentrate on any sort of Bible reading. I was tormented within my soul. I felt distant from God and I couldn't understand why He allowed this entire situation to happen. I wanted to keep trusting Him, knowing He had the bigger picture in mind and that He has the power to work all thing together for good as one of my favorite Bible verses reminded me from Romans 8:28. But I felt like my faith was being rocked and hit hard. Though I don't think I voiced it to anyone, I was seriously wondering if I was going to be able to endure and keep trusting in Him. This whole devastation had been so awful and I couldn't understand why He allowed it not only to happen, but allow me to be such an intricate part of it all. I wished so much none of it happened and we could turn back the time and have none of these devastating events happen one after another.

But they did.

Each one happened and God was watching from heaven as each person crossed over the avalanche, from one side to the other. He saw Clive and Lawrence put their bodies face down when the massive flow of rocks fell, and He saw that huge boulder hit Keiko dead-on, knocking her from the tree branch she was clutching. Why had He allowed for each one of these events to happen as they did? And why was I buried as I was, with my head bent downward and my arms and fingers stretched heavenward, providing the air pocket and even slight movement of my fingers under the rocks? I constantly asked why was I granted life and why were they given death?

I know everyone is given a time to die. As one of my teammates, Elizabeth, had reminded, in Proverbs, a book of the Bible known for its profound wisdom, God says, "Many are the plans in a man's heart, but it is the Lord's purpose that prevails" (19:21). In Proverbs 16:33 we read, "The lot is cast into the lap, but its every decision is from the Lord." Based on these verses and what I knew personally about God, He was ultimately in control of all things.

Yet why did He allow these things to happen in this way? Was He really good, and all-wise and all-loving? I wrestled within my heart, soul and mind to find answers to these questions. I wondered to myself, will I indeed walk and carry on with the Lord? I had been through so many trials in my past, divorced parents, an alcoholic father, rage, more divorce and more unhappiness, and yet for the past 20 years of being a Christian, I never turned away from God even though life's devastation was nearly crippling and unbearable at times. In all these past situations, I could see a fairly clear link between people's decisions and their consequences.

This time, however, I could see no clear cause for such tragic effects. The mountain accident was so baffling to me because I couldn't see it as the effect of anyone's wrong or bad decision. I couldn't help but wonder deep within what choice I would make. Even if I did not understand — and might never under-stand — the accident, would I continue to choose to trust and believe in God? This was a deep residing question within my soul and I felt terrified even to voice these thoughts to anyone.

A couple days later, in the beginning of the third week at home, Elliot, my teammate and good friend for the past year and a half, came over. Elliot had already come over a couple of times in the past two weeks to give me medicine for my joints and to pray. The first time he visited, I was not home, but he left me a note with a significant quote by St. Ignatius (1491–1556): "If God causes you to suffer much, it is a sign that He has great designs for you, and that He certainly intends to make you a saint. And if you wish to become a great saint, entreat Him yourself to give you much opportu-nity for suffering; for there is no wood better to kindle the fire of holy love than the wood of the cross, which Christ used for His own great sacrifice of boundless charity."

I wanted to ask him more about this quote's meaning and why he left it for me. He told me he did not want to just say, "Get well soon," which implies, "It will be okay" or, "You'll be alright." Too often, those statements can trivialize the moment. This quote from St. Ignatius was something he felt I needed to hear, mainly because it put my experience in the right Christian context. The avalanche was not just "a bad thing that happened," but a pivotal part of my life with God.

"You've been burned with suffering," Elliot said, "and because it's so intense, it is clear that God has a greater design for you. I just didn't want you to lose sight of that, God's Providence."

After he shared this with me, I remember distinctly I started voicing my own inner thoughts with him. He has an intimate walk with the Lord, and for as long as I had known him, we had been able to talk deeply and freely about spiritual matters. I felt I could open up with him about the more important matters of my heart and soul and I felt free to voice the questions and struggles I was having.

I guess I had always felt somewhat guarded with others I had talked to about the accident since I felt indirectly from some of them that I was supposed to move on with life, and off and away from the mountain. But, just as my sister had mentioned in regards to PTSD, I couldn't stop myself from thinking about each event that occurred on the mountain. No matter how much I may have wanted to return to everyday life, I felt disabled and incapable of functioning normally. The thoughts, emotions and pain remained stuck in my heart and I had many questions about all of it.

As I began talking with Elliot, I felt a freedom come over me to release my bottled up emotions. It wasn't as if I was making much sense with what I was speaking, but just trying to express it and let it out was comforting in and of itself. I began to cry and I sensed from Elliot, it was okay. It was okay to cry and it was okay to voice my confusion and questions.

Elliot sat down next to me and after listening to me, asked if he could pray for me. My heart had been vulnerable with Jesus about my questions and feelings in the past week, so that at this moment, when I joined in prayer with Elliot, I was able to give myself into Jesus' arms. I was in a desperate state and I needed God sincerely. I wanted to pray and I knew I was in need of prayer. When Elliot prayed I was able to agree with every one of Elliot's heart felt cries for inner healing and for God's presence to overwhelm me and flood over me.

After we finished praying, since I had told Elliot that one of my struggles was being unable to read, comprehend or be touched by reading the Bible, he volunteered to come over in the next couple days to read to me. This idea had never occurred to me before, but I believed there was power in hearing the word of God spoken out loud. I thought maybe if I sat down, without trying to do or feel something, but just simply be a receiver and hearer of God's Word, then maybe that would indeed be good for my heart. Elliot decided to come over two days later on Wednesday. The same night he had chosen, I also had invited Bonnie over to my house for dinner so I could talk with her and ask her for more understanding to some questions I had had about the accident. Since Elliot was also friends with her, I thought it would be a perfect night for him to come.

When Bonnie did come over, we ended up having a very meaningful talk. She explained many more of the details of what had happened to the group after the avalanche, as well as her own emotions and thoughts. Since she had sat by my side nearly the entire night in the mountain house after the avalanche, it was very comforting to talk with her and hear from her heart of that night's events. She too was struggling with memories and scenes which flashed through her head, but she told me how she kept praying for God's hand of comfort and help to strengthen her. I told her of my inability to read God's Word and that Elliot was coming over to read to me. She thought that was a great idea and decided to stay to wait for him also, not only for my sake, but for her sake, too.

Elliot arrived shortly thereafter and though I didn't know what he should read, he chose to read Psalm 18.

1 I love you, O LORD, my strength.

2 The LORD is my rock, my fortress and my deliverer;
my God is my rock, in whom I take refuge.
He is my shield and the horn of my salvation, my stronghold.

3 I call to the LORD, who is worthy of praise,
 and I am saved from my enemies.

4 The cords of death entangled me;
 the torrents of destruction overwhelmed me.

5 The cords of the grave coiled around me;
the snares of death confronted me.

6 In my distress I called to the LORD;
I cried to my God for help.
From his temple he heard my voice;
my cry came before him, into his ears.

7 The earth trembled and quaked,
and the foundations of the mountains shook;
they trembled because he was angry.

8 Smoke rose from his nostrils;
consuming fire came from his mouth,
burning coals blazed out of it.

9 He parted the heavens and came down;
dark clouds were under his feet.

10 He mounted the cherubim and flew;
he soared on the wings of the wind.

11 He made darkness his covering, his canopy around him—
the dark rain clouds of the sky.

12 Out of the brightness of his presence clouds advanced,
with hailstones and bolts of lightning.

13 The LORD thundered from heaven;
the voice of the Most High resounded.

14 He shot his arrows and scattered the enemies ,
great bolts of lightning and routed them.

15 The valleys of the sea were exposed
and the foundations of the earth laid bare
at your rebuke, O LORD,
at the blast of breath from your nostrils.

16 He reached down from on high and took hold of me;
he drew me out of deep waters.

17 He rescued me from my powerful enemy,
from my foes, who were too strong for me.

18 They confronted me in the day of my disaster,
but the LORD was my support.

19 He brought me out into a spacious place;
he rescued me because he delighted in me.

In the past, it was one of my favorite psalms. But now, for some reason, its words sprang to new life. Words and phrases grabbed my heart and mind with a surprisingly vivid intensity. The cords of death *entangle* me — the cords of the grave *coil around me* — in my distress, I call to the Lord and He hears my cry — He parts the heavens and *comes down* to rescue me — He reaches down from on high and rescues me from my powerful enemy.

As Elliot read verse after verse, and as he began to tell the story of God's deliverance, I imagined the Lord arising and fleeing down to rescue me, imagining how He did everything to make a way to reach me. I could clearly see Him coming out of the brightness, with bolts of lightning advancing and making a way to the earth, for *me*. I think this imagery was so moving, and God's Word was so powerful again after weeks of darkness, because the Lord became as vivid in my mind as my memories of the avalanche were. For weeks, I could imagine nothing more stark than the tumbling rocks, the pouring rain, and the cold darkness, but now at last something greater was just as vivid in my mind.

As Elliot read God's truth and His Word was beginning to come alive in my heart, I noticed how it started to penetrate my heart. I was hearing such descriptive words of His love and care and as I just listened, and did nothing more, but allow myself to soak in His truth, I was being touched.

Elliot read it two times to me and then read some other passages from the Bible. I felt this was good for me since it was the first time since the accident the Words of God were coming off the pages straight into my heart. It was as if the rocks around my heart were being removed one at a time as I heard the Scriptures one word at a time. At the Banner church service, I had felt my head unearthed, though within a day I was painfully aware of how oppressed and vulnerable I still was. Now as I felt my heart being freed and exposed to the light of God's love, it felt as liberating as when my torso and arms had been unearthed. In this short hour, I didn't feel completely changed or healed immediately; my legs were still buried, so to speak. It wasn't a complete transformation, but I knew many rocks had been moved off my heart. God was stirring my insides and I felt His presence in a newer and deeper way.

The next day, Thursday, after lunch and a physical therapy appointment, I was scheduled to go to Banner church at 3:00 P.M. for more prayer. Pastor Samuel's wife, Pastor May and Vincent's wife, Maggie, were going to pray for me. They can speak English well, but since they felt more comfortable praying in Chinese, Linda came in to translate for them in English. As they prayed for me, they wanted me just to sit still quietly before God as they waited on God for any impressions or words they might feel from Him.

Soon after they began praying, they began speaking many words that resonated within my heart. One of them said I had a wall around my heart and my emotions couldn't be expressed. But I needed to have that wall be broken down. They said those things I don't understand, I need to surrender to God and let Him control. He is God.

One of them also spoke for quite some time about God's love. She told me that God is love and though I teach about God's love to others, I myself needed to experience it like never before. She said no eye, nor ear or heart can explain it, but God wants me to experience this love of His even deeper. She said though His love can be explained to me, He now wants to *show* me His love.

One of them went on to say that she saw a picture in her mind of a Bible closed on the table. Though the Bible was closed, Jesus was saying to me, "I am here." When she said this, it really spoke to me because I had indeed felt the Bible's meaning was closed to me ever since the accident occurred. It was comforting to know He was indeed with me, despite my ongoing numbness to His Presence and deafness to His Word.

She went on to say God too is sad and sorrowful, but I need to have faith and hold on right now. She said I was questioning, "Will I still follow God?" And then she asked me, "Do you trust Him? Have you lost confidence in God? Do you believe He was with you?"

She paused, but then said, in the future I will understand many words from Him; but my heart isn't able to hear or understand them now. I do need to hold on, and have faith. He wants to nourish my heart and He wants to hold me like a crying baby.

One of them also saw a picture in her mind of a clam with a pearl in it; through the storms, sand inside kept refining it into a beautiful pearl. Though I pass through the valley of death, there is hope for a resurrection and though I can't see it, He will give a victory and that is a promise. There will be a resurrection of goodness, kindness and grace. He will raise me up and make me strong. I just need to rest now, not struggle or worry, because it is Jesus' work. He is refining me.

I left church that day uplifted in some ways, encouraged by the words and images I had heard, and yet I still felt sorrow and deep pain residing in my heart. It was undeniably hard to understand why all this had happened and why I had been a part of this hiking accident. I just needed to wait on God and trust that His promises would indeed come to pass. I needed to take one day at a time and believe in God's provision of healing along the way.

~ ✛ ~

The following day, on Friday, June 3, exactly three weeks after the accident, I visited Shaowsy with Bonnie and Maggie, Vincent's wife. For the first week after the accident I had been in the same hospital as Shaowsy, and though I tried everyday to see her, she was always out of her room getting treatments. Maggie drove me up to her house and I was finally able to meet with her. She had been home for a couple weeks now, and, like me, doing physical therapy everyday. Since she had been buried for so many hours, nerves in her legs and one arm were seriously damaged. The doctors said they would grow back in six months but she was in considerable pain.

When I arrived at her house, I was overcome with emotion. I was so thankful to see her walking, though limping and on crutches, yet I was also sad to see her in such pain. It was nice to be in her house, sitting on her cushioned couches, seeing her smiling face. She didn't look nearly as bad as I imagined she would and her countenance seemed good.

We talked at length about the time of the avalanche and how right before the rocks fell, she looked back and saw Clive and Lawrence put their heads down to the ground. Because I was directly behind her about five to ten feet, she never knew I was there until only after she heard me being unburied. It was amazing for me to talk to someone who shared so many of the same experiences. She had been buried up to her chin, unable to move, so scared of more falling rocks and, like me, had been hit hard on the head when the second cascade of rocks came down. Though I had talked briefly with others who had been in the hiking accident, my experience was quite different from theirs. With Shaowsy, however, we could relate to each other in many key ways, and because of this it was good to spend time together, sharing with each other.

One reason I had wanted to see her so badly was to apologize to her. All night long I struggled with not unburying her and I wanted to sincerely apologize to her for not helping her more.

As soon as I spoke these words, I was startled by her response. She told me she had no ill feelings towards me and did not blame me for anything. My eyes instantly welled up with tears; I was touched deeply by her reply. I told her I was a Christian and I told her I believed in Jesus and though I was physically unable to help her that night, I prayed for her all night long. I prayed one prayer for her in particular all night over and over again and that was for God to protect her and not have one rock hit her in the exposed and unprotected area she was half buried in. Though I was deeply relieved she had not ever been hit, and I was indeed thankful to God, I had felt badly in my heart for a long time for not doing more for her.

Shaowsy completely released me through her words and actions towards me. She looked into my eyes and held onto my hand while she spoke; I knew she was being honest with me. She wanted me to be free and carry no feelings of guilt. My heart was moved and greatly touched by this conversation and all that we shared in it. Before we left, Maggie, Bonnie and I all prayed for her for quite some time and though she didn't believe in Jesus, she expressed her sincere appreciation for our concern and prayers for her. That evening as Maggie and Bonnie drove me home, despite how liberating the time with Shaowsy had been, I wept deeply, uncontrollably, overwhelmed once more by all the events and emotions this avalanche had generated.

A day later, Friday, I continued on with my normal schedule of physical therapy and lunch with some of the SRAM folks. That night I had my Bible study with the Taiwanese at church and since I had shared much of my heart with Bonnie in the past couple of days, she strongly recommended that I ask for prayer from the group that night. I wanted to continue the

Bible study through the gospel of John and though I still hadn't experienced much depth in the Word yet, I wanted us to keep studying as we had planned. We had a good discussion and I felt God was indeed guiding and leading us with His Holy Spirit as we pondered and talked about Jesus' words. After the study, Bonnie encouraged the group to gather around me and pray for me and my healing. I didn't feel completely comfortable asking for this, since I didn't know everyone in the group that well, so I added if anyone needed to go home, they were free to leave, while those that could stay, could remain. Some did leave, but about eight Taiwanese ladies stood by my side to pray for me.

Bonnie prayed first and then several others followed her lead. All who prayed truly spoke to God from their hearts, sincerely agonizing and crying out to God on my behalf for His healing touch. Their hearts of love and concern for me were especially evident. I could feel the levels of hardness eroding away in my heart, softened by the Lord's presence. I began to cry and within minutes I was sobbing and my entire upper body was shaking. I felt I was releasing the depth of my pain in a newer way than I had ever done before and I didn't try to control how hard I sobbed. I just surrendered and cried as I needed to cry. The pain was there, the unanswered questions were there and the doubts towards God were there. I didn't want to pretend they weren't there, and I didn't want to hold back the depth of these inner struggles and feelings.

After they prayed for me, I began to pray out loud also. I had felt each one of these women's love for me and I felt free before them to express the depth of my heart and pain. As I cried and sobbed, I told God how hard this whole thing was for me. I told Him I wished it had never happened. I told Him my heart was breaking and I felt so sad about Keiko, Lawrence and Clive. Then I just cried silently and many of the ladies were crying silently also.

I then began to speak aloud again and for the first time, I verbally told God though I didn't want to, I was doubting Him. I was doubting why all these things had to happen as they did. I told Him I wanted to trust Him, but I was having such a tough time doing so. It was hard to confess this, but after I prayed, I began to feel a burden being lifted off my back. It was as if through this confession, the heavy rocks of guilt, confusion, pain, and doubt were being gently lifted away. I had needed to verbally acknowledge my doubt and lack of trust in His sovereign plan. I had needed to relinquish my heart to God and be honest about my struggles. I had needed to pray and cry before Him. There is something powerful about honest confession before others and before God and as I did this, I started to experience a freedom I hadn't yet felt.

We closed in prayer and I stayed to talk with several of the ladies for another hour or so. They asked if I was feeling better, and though I wanted to answer with a definite yes, I only responded, "It was very good to pray." I knew it had been good to pray and I had felt some release of burden from my soul, but I didn't know how to express it in words at that moment. I just knew it had been good for me to confess my inner doubt and break the power of that secret before others and God.

I went home that night, went to bed and fell asleep. When I awoke on Saturday, I awoke with something literally lifted off of my soul. I cannot explain it, nor do I want to make light of it, but something sincerely had happened to me. For a complete three weeks, I had felt so heavy, so burdened, so plagued with pain, depression, confusion and doubt. And when I awoke that morning, it was as if a release or a break-through had happened. I at last felt I had been unburied from the darkness that had shrouded my heart. I felt at peace for the first time since the accident. I felt a new-found closeness to God; I could talk to Him again and be close to Him. It was as if I was coming back to life and I was indeed being resurrected from the dead. The cords of death were severed and cast off me; I was a prisoner set free, finally set free from head to toe. It was and is to this day one of the most amazing supernatural experiences I have ever encountered.

I had been so close to death and I had felt it with every fiber of my being. There was no escaping the fact that three of my dear students had died. Agonized by survivor's guilt, I could not help thinking about them every day, and nearly every minute, grieving for each of them over the past three weeks. Plus, my own doubt and lack of trust in God's sovereignty had plagued me to the core of my being.

But when I awoke that morning, I felt as if I had been reborn, as if I had come to life again. I could live again and I did not need to feel guilty for it.

The entire day I felt this new sense of freedom and I couldn't help but marvel at the difference of emotions and feelings. It was as if I wanted to see if indeed it was true and real. I wanted to shake myself so hard and see if it would change or come off of me, but it did not. That new sense of life remained and from that day forward, though, yes, I have still many, many times grieved deeply in my heart for all the events that did happen up on that mountain, the cords of death and entanglement seemed to be released off of me. It was simply a miracle and one I will probably marvel at for the rest of my life since it was such a dramatic change.

After this amazing event, since the feelings never did leave me, the month of June seemed easier to handle. I still had to go to physical therapy daily and I continued to sorrow over the death of the others, but there was a peaceful freedom within that enabled me to carry on with renewed hope. I slowly gained strength in my leg and I began to walk with a crutch, which in turn allowed me to get back on my scooter and resume my work duties. It was great to be independent and on a somewhat normal schedule again. Having been dependent on other people for so many weeks had weighed down on me. It was so refreshing to do things on my own again, like I finally had my legs back and they were no longer paralyzed by the burden of rocks. By June, I was indeed liberated physically and emotionally. It was a pivotal month not only for my body and soul, but also for some key relationships in my life. Two events that stand out in this month were what I would call divine encounters. Out of the debris and ashes God was bringing new life. I was about to meet two people who would be God's provision of comfort and encouragement, as flowers bursting forth from the wasteland.

Amanda had been taking Chinese classes for over a year and she and her teacher Mattie were talking about the hiking accident when they realized they were both indirectly involved. Amanda found out that Mattie was the cousin of Lawrence and Mattie found out I was a good friend of Amanda's. They both marveled at this coincidence and connection. What made matters even more amazing is that Mattie is a Christian and had felt so burdened for Lawrence's family and she wanted desperately to share God's love and comfort with them. Amanda knew that was also my desire and thought how wonderful it would be if both of us could meet and talk.

When Amanda told me of this encounter with Mattie, my eyes immediately welled up with tears. Not only was Mattie a Christian, but she was able to speak English fluently. So if and when we did talk with Lawrence's family, she could translate for me and we could share with Lawrence's family having the same mind frame and heart. I got her phone number and set up a time we could meet and visit Lawrence's family. I wanted to bring a gift to his family, visit them in their home and talk with each of the family members individually.

As expected, the time at their home was bittersweet. It was good to meet the entire family, listen to their hearts and hear of their stories, but it was also extremely painful. All of us, often throughout our conversations, would start crying at some moment. Lawrence's two sisters, one older and one younger, talked openly with me and we had a nice rapport from that day forward. My heart broke with theirs and as Mattie and I both talked with them, I believe they saw how much I cared. When Mattie and I asked if we could pray for them, they consented. Several times during my prayer, I couldn't help crying. I wanted desperately for Jesus to comfort them and touch their extremely wounded hearts.

After that first encounter, Lawrence's sisters, Mattie, and I met several times afterward for more sharing, talking and praying. They wanted to hear every detail of the accident each time we met. I'm sure, due to their own grieving and suffering, only parts of the story were heard and understood when I shared since they could only take in so much at a time. Thus, I ended up repeating the story each time I met with them. Sometimes we met at a coffee shop, a couple times they came to Banner church for the service, but always when we met, we prayed together. Those were agonizing times. It was as if at those times, when we stilled our hearts and minds and felt our pain, that the sorrow was heaviest. Many tears were shed and all we could do was to continue to ask God for His healing touch.

Months passed and we didn't see each other. I went back to the States and after I came back, there was still no contact. But at the one year mark, I contacted Mattie again and asked her if she would visit Lawrence's family with me. We decided to go over before the anniversary of May 12th and ended up going on May 7th in the late afternoon. Mattie called the family to tell them we were coming.

Immediately when I entered their shop and saw their faces, I was so grateful I had come; it was good to see them again. I cared for them deeply. Though I hadn't seen them for such a long time, I instantly re-connected with them in my heart. We sat down together, drank tea and talked for hours. They told me many stories of the past year and how they were coping with life.

In particular, one story they told me was that according to the Lunar calendar, May 2nd was the one year mark of Lawrence's death. They asked me if I remembered that day because it was a day of torrential rain. I instantly remembered because I had been sitting in my apartment that day, staring out the window and going over the events of the accident in my mind. The pouring rain triggered my memories and I sat on my sofa for a long time reminiscing and contemplating life. Lawrence's mom reminded me that on May 1st it had been a beautiful clear sunny day. Yet on Tuesday, May 2nd, there were sudden downpours. Lawrence's family was going to the temple that day to make sacrifices and prayers for him and as they were on their way, as the rain was pouring down, they couldn't help but feel that Lawrence was saying to them, "I remember you."

I began crying. What an astonishing thing to happen on that exact day, the one-year mark. I felt the depth of pain flood over me all over again as they conveyed this story to me. There was such deep sadness, sorrow and remorse, and not having answers made it difficult.

They then relayed another interesting insight. The Chinese culture believes numbers have significance and meaning. For example, there are lucky days due to the implication of the numbers. Unfortunately, there are also unlucky numbers. Lawrence's dad told me that Keiko was 26 years old, Lawrence was 29 and Clive was 32 and each of them were separated by sets of three, and this was bad luck. They felt it was "their destiny" due to the significance of the numbers. I just listened quietly, but then Lawrence's younger sister said to me it was absolutely amazing I was alive. She said that what saved me was the fact that my hands weren't behind my head, but up so I could extend them and move the rocks. I was at a loss for words. I have wondered a thousand times why Lawrence and the others had died and I was alive. I sat in silence then, and I sit in silence now.

Before I left their place, I asked if I could pray for them all again. I wanted Jesus to comfort and help them continually. It was a special time to lift our hearts to God and cry together once again. I left their place saddened, but as I talked with Mattie over dinner, I was encouraged by her own love for them, desire to help them and be a blessing to them. Talking with Mattie helped me once again entrust Lawrence's family unto God.

At the end of June, only a month after the accident, the second divine encounter I had was with a lady at the physical therapy office. My own personal doctor, Mr. Yang, could speak English fairly well, but he also had another patient, Melanie, who could speak English very well. She evidently was interested in me and knowing why I was there in the hospital every day.

After several weeks she finally approached me and started talking. Usually, I have a tendency to not be very talkative with total strangers. In fact, I tend to keep the conversations quite short. But this time, every time she asked me a question, I kept talking in great detail not only about the accident and God supernaturally providing a way for me to survive, but also about my recent experience with prayer. I expressed to her that though I had not died in the accident, it was as if I had died emotionally or spiritually. But God, in His great mercy, had not only spared my life physically, He also gave me new life and freedom within my heart. It was strange for me to share so openly and transparently with this lady, but I felt like I couldn't help but keep sharing with her. As I spoke, she just continued listening, nodding at various times and following me around the physical therapy office as I went from one table to the next, doing my various exercises. We must have talked for an hour that first day and at the end of our conversation, she kept repeating, "Oh, this was so interesting. It was so good to talk to you."

The following days we continued talking, and again I did something I usually never do. She told me she had a daughter named Alice who just finished senior high school and was entering the university in September. Melanie asked if over the summer months I could tutor her daughter. While living in Taiwan, I have been asked this question countless times and my answer is usually the same, No. I have enough work and I don't want to meet with another person and do one-on-one teaching on my off time.

But this time, I not only responded with a favorable answer, but when she asked me where we could have classes, I responded we could possibly do it in my own home. I couldn't believe what was coming out of my mouth; I had never given a response like that before and basically Melanie and I were still strangers.

I remember going home that afternoon and telling my roommate Carrie, "The strangest thing happened to me today!"

Carrie's response was great. She said to me, "Maybe God is doing something and He wants you to get to know the two of them."

I only uttered, "Maybe," since I was still so surprised at my own response.

Over the summer months, I did in fact teach Alice at my home, and Melanie would always drop her off before the lessons and pick her up when we were finished. I would speak briefly with Melanie at those times, but mostly we became friends in the physical therapy office. It soon became evident that Melanie as well as Alice, were looking for more meaning to life. Melanie shared with me how she had gone to the Buddhist temple nearly her entire life, but never felt or experienced anything from her god. Yet, after hearing my story, she couldn't help but wonder about my God. I told her about my English Bible study at Banner church for Taiwanese and at the end of July, she and Alice started attending faithfully.

It has been an amazing journey to watch both Alice and, especially, Melanie be transformed before my eyes. Melanie has been coming nearly every single week for the past year and a half as we studied the Gospels of Luke and John.

When Melanie and I talked recently, she told me over and over again, what a miracle it was that we met in that physical therapy office. Though her major was English literature and she had read much of the Bible before, she had never understood it, nor felt anything from it. But each week, while we met at church and discussed as a group the meaning of Jesus' words and actions, she came to understand Him better and better.

She then told me, what's more, over the past year when we prayed together for her, our prayers were answered and she experienced so many miracles in her life. She had looked and wanted an English teaching position and was trying desperately to find a job anywhere in Taiwan. But when our group prayed for her, we prayed specifically she would find a good job in her own city, right here in Taichung, so she would not need to leave her daughters. Not only did God give her miracles when He helped her to successfully pass her English tests, but she got a teaching position for one year at an elementary school, which happened to be only one block from my home. As she relayed this information to me, she repeatedly said that God was becoming so real to her, because He "noticed" her.

"In all of my years of going to the Buddhist temple," she explained, "the majority of the time, I did not feel anything, and in fact, I felt like I was being ignored."

She then said that when we prayed to Jesus, she felt, "He not only is interested in me, and He *notices* me, but He grants our requests."

She was so touched by this truth that she couldn't help but recite the words, "He notices me," over and over again. That reality had profoundly impacted her and she now realizes that God is close to her and He really loves her.

Meeting both Melanie and Mattie has once again revealed to me that out of despair, darkness, and sorrow, God can and does bring comfort, hope, and love. These two ladies were for me beautiful flowers that arose out of the ashes.

After the summer, I was finally able to go home to California in October of 2005 to visit my family and friends for the first time since the accident. By this time, though only five months had passed, I was able to walk fairly comfortably, though I needed to wear a knee brace continually throughout the day. My physical therapy doctor told me I needed to do home exercises and try to bike, walk, and swim as much as I could to continue to make the muscles around my knee strong.

The first week home I stayed with my mother and it was there that God worked very significantly in my life. I had picked up a book about prayer by Jim Cymbala off her bookshelf and every night before bed I would read a chapter. On the third night, though it was late, I wanted to finish the chapter about God answering prayers in the midst of tragedy. In the latter part of the chapter, Cymbala relays a story about a woman who gives a personal testimony and first hand account of her own tragedy. She herself had been in the World Trade Center on the day of 9/11 when the planes crashed into them. Her office was up on the 64th floor, and after the sudden crash, commotion, and panic, she, along with her fellow co-workers, ran down every flight of stairs to try and reach safety at the bottom.

She describes in detail what it was like running down, seeing the smoke, hearing the noises, and passing fire fighters who were going up the stairs. But when she arrived at the 13th floor, the building crashed down all around her and she was literally buried alive. She had cement all around her; she was completely pinned down, but she was still conscious.

As I read, I immediately began to cry. Someone else had been buried alive and was telling her own personal story! She described her emotions of not knowing if someone would find her, of not being able to move a single part of her body, and of praying out desperately to God. I could relate to everything she wrote! She then described how she had been raised a Catholic, but had fallen away from her faith. But at this moment, she cried out desperately to Jesus and resolutely decided in her heart again, to follow Him.

Her story goes on to describe how she was miraculously saved and delivered (I'll let you read the book for yourself!), and how she was taken to the hospital and recovered for months afterward. Once her friends started visiting her in the hospital, they commented on how matted her hair was due to the dust and debris which completely coated and covered it. Again, I could relate so well since my own hair had been covered with mud and pebbles and had taken days to clean out!

She was the only survivor of those whom she had run down the stairs with and though like me, didn't understand why she was alive and the others dead, she resolved in her heart to follow Jesus. Her personal testimony of sorrow and tragedy, while experiencing the graciousness and power of God was clearly revealed throughout each one of the pages.

I was deeply touched and when I finished the chapter, I put the book down on the bed and sobbed for a long time. I couldn't believe I was reading a book, my first book while home, with a story so intimately similar to my own experience of the past five months. God was so real and kind to allow me to read such an account. I knew this was no coincidence and once again surrendered myself to Him and to His will and plan for my life.

In a few days, on Sunday, my mother had invited me to speak at her seniors' group at church. A couple hundred people were present and they gave me about 30 minutes to speak. I shared briefly with them about my personal decision to follow Christ, where and what I had done since I decided to follow Him, and how I had been led to Taiwan. I shared for approximately half the time about the hiking accident and described the miracles God had brought me through. I openly cried as I shared my story for the first time in front of a large crowd. I had been powerfully moved by God in countless ways that I couldn't hold back sharing my experience of Him with those dear old people.

The pastor, Jim Smoke, came up to me afterward and told me I needed to take this story of mine and write it into a book. I stared at him dumbfounded. He said that this story was a miracle and though I had suffered greatly, God had allowed me to overcome and persevere with Him. He urged me to share with others the mercies of God and how by holding onto Him, we can prevail. I am not a writer, nor had I ever imagined writing a book, but I tucked this bit of advice within my heart and pondered it.

Over the following weeks, I shared my story with pastors at two separate churches and after I finished speaking, they also each urged me to write this story as a book. Three pastors speaking the same word to me within a matter of weeks greatly impacted me. Was this indeed something God was directing me towards?

And yet, as I thought about the lady who was buried under the World Trade Center and how my heart burned within me as I was reading of her own account, I couldn't help but wonder if my story, like hers, would be an inspiration to others. Her story, like mine, was about lives being lost while those who survive have to press on. Not just to press on and survive, but press on to overcome the tragedy and *keep trusting* and holding onto God. Most certainly, her life, as well as mine, had been forever changed as a result of traumatic events. I would never be the same person I was before the accident.

~ + ~

More than a year has passed since meeting with the pastors in America (in October 2005), and I did indeed take the words of my pastor friends to heart. During 2006, I worked steadily on finishing this book. I interviewed several people who were involved in this accident and I heard first account stories I had never heard before. Many times while talking with these people, I would cry as I listened to their own personal suffering and trauma. Each story told was from a different perspective and each relayed sights they had seen, sorrow they had suffered, and pain they had endured.

One person expressed that he never wanted to go hiking again and I knew this was indeed a real fear. I myself have experienced fear and know how it can incapacitate. But I have also heard that in order to overcome fear, one must face that fear and go through it in order to get to the other side. I knew I also needed to overcome my fear; I needed to go on one more hiking trip in Taiwan so that I would not be over-come with fear and sink back down into it.

During my first hike with SRAM in 2004, when we hiked to Jamin Lake, we had hiked some of the highest peaks of Taiwan, a small island with about two hundred peaks taller than 3,000 meters (approximately 10,000 feet). When we reached one of the summits, a guide told us that across the way from us was the highest peak in Taiwan, Jade Mountain. From the moment I saw that peak, I had an insatiable desire to climb it. I knew one day I would have to do it.

In October 2006, a good friend of mine, named Calvin, invited me to go on a hiking trip to Jade Mountain. I was excited, yet nervous, when he invited me. He told me that near the summit of the mountain, there is a cabin, which can only hold 100 people. Every weekend there is a lottery for which hiking groups can go.

Finally, on October 21st and 22nd, Calvin and I were drawn in the lottery and were accepted within one group. I told Calvin I wanted to go, but I was also scared to take another excursion. He continually reassured me that we would be safe and I could even lead the pace for us and our group. He strongly desired to help me overcome all my fears and make it to the top peak of Taiwan, Jade Mountain!

On October 21st, at 5:30 A.M. Calvin picked me up on his motor bike and drove me through the dimly lit streets of Taichung to meet our guide at his van. As I was sitting on the back of the motor bike, I told Calvin how nervous I was and when he asked me why, I said, "I want to come back alive."

He answered and said with absolute confidence and assurance, "We are going to come back alive!"

There wasn't any question in his mind that we'd come back alive; he knew we would. It was the same assurance Josh had spoken to me throughout that night waiting in the rain, waiting for our rescue. Now, on my way up a new mountain, I needed to hold onto God and trust Him with the outcome once again.

We arrived to the mountain base around 9:00 A.M. and I was extremely nervous. I kept wondering to myself, "What will this mountain be like? Will it be too steep? Will I be able to climb it, and not just physically, but emotionally too?"

As we prepped our bags and waited on the others in our group, I went to the toilet several times. (Did I mention I was nervous?) Thankfully, after we geared up, within minutes of walking, we stopped at the visitor's center where we were instructed to watch a video on the hike. As I watched, I saw that it was a relatively easy trail, which really calmed me down and I was able to breathe a deep sigh of relief. I realized I didn't need to be so terrified and I could relax. Before this trip, I had prayed many times asking God if I should indeed go on this hike and each time I prayed, I felt a strong yes. I had felt His assurance and peace each time I prayed and

I now felt it again while I watched the video. I just needed to trust Him.

As we began our climb and I could see the trail ahead of me, I saw the sunny crystal clear blue skies. I felt confidence and joy arising within me. It was like a surge of faith was being stirred deep within my heart and soul and I had assurance that God was indeed going to take care of me.

The hike up was beautiful, not very strenuous and there were only a few places where the road narrowed so that the edge of our path was close to our feet. These moments sent a chill through my entire body since I could see the drop-offs, but thankfully none of them were more than 50 meters. I forced myself to look them square on and I was able to look down. As I gazed downward though, I realized even if I did fall into one of them, I would most likely only get injured, since the drop-offs were not nearly as steep as at Tun Yuan Mountain, where we had hiked in Puli. I was trying to rationalize all of this so that when I did look down at these cliffs, by the grace of God, I could try to face my fears of the mountain.

After we hiked about eight kilometers, we arrived to the mountain cabin at around 4:00 P.M. I was happy to be there and thankfully I wasn't that exhausted, but because we were already over 10,000 feet in elevation, I was experiencing a terrible headache. I had never had altitude sickness before, but as the night wore on I was feeling dizzy and in great pain. As I lay down, I prayed to God many times. I wanted to make it to the peak in the morning, but I needed a miracle of healing for my head. After a couple hours, Calvin found a doctor because not only was I sick, but one of our partners on the team was sick also. He got medicine for us, and thankfully we all finally fell asleep for a few hours. We awoke at 2:30 A.M. and I was feeling remarkably fine.

After a quick breakfast, we started our ascent. Calvin had told me earlier that week that on October 21st there was supposed to be a meteor shower. As we hiked up the switch-

backs, our guide often had us stop for a few minutes to rest.
At every break, I would gaze up into the dark night sky, and
I saw at least ten shooting stars on our way up to the peak.
They were spectacular and each time I saw one, I once again
felt the love, mercy and care of God's gracious hand upon
me. Each shooting star was a sign to me that God was indeed
watching out for me and did care for me intimately.

The last section of the climb to the peak was the steepest
section and in order to arrive at the top, we had to grab onto
ropes which were fastened with metal bars along the path. We
made it to the peak right before sunrise and watched the most
glorious sunrise I have ever seen. Tons of mountain peaks
could be seen all around us and as the sun shone its brilliant
rays, we were mesmerized by its splendor. We had indeed
made it and there was such a feeling of relief and accomplish-
ment when we sat down and observed the beauty all about us.

After we took many pictures, we started our descent, had a big brunch at the mountain cabin, and hiked downwards to the van till mid-afternoon.

Arriving in Taichung, alive and well, was awesome. I had such a deep peace and gratefulness to God for bringing both Calvin and me through a great experience. I will be forever appreciative to Jesus for that trip, not only for helping me to face and overcome my fears, but allowing me to experience such depth of beauty and majesty all around me and more importantly, within my soul. God is indeed my Helper, my Deliverer, and my ROCK!

EPILOGUE

~ + ~

Though I have been living in Taiwan for just over three years, and will be leaving in less than a month, in no way has this experience of the avalanche stifled or hindered me from moving forward with God's plans for me. Though I have suffered greatly from this traumatic event, and my world was indeed rocked, tragedy has only served to refine my vision as I follow after my Lord and Savior Jesus Christ. The entire experience has not only broadened and deepened the call of God on my life, but has also allowed me to dream to newer and greater heights. I was not only unburied from the physical darkness of thousands of rocks all around me, but also resurrected from the emotional and spiritual oppression of guilt and doubt. As a result I feel a greater sense of purpose and worth towards life than ever before. God has given me renewed vision to go further and live more deeply for Him.

The cords of death, the chains of bondage, and the utter darkness of confusion *can be overcome* in and through Jesus. Jesus has not granted me mere "resuscitation" back to where I was before, but *resurrection* from the grave to a new level of Christ-likeness. Through Christ our saving rock, we not only can recover from tragedy but can also dream and live again in fullness of hope and faith.

Climb with me and hold on to the Rock which saves!

THIS IS CLOSE TO THE AREA IN WHICH I WAS BURIED AND THE TYPE OF DEBRIS I WAS UNDER.

TERRI, SAM (THE ONE WHO BECAME A BELIEVER IN CHRIST AS A RESULT OF THIS ACCIDENT), AND JOSH (THE ONE WHO UNBURIED ME)

**TERRI AND CALVIN AT SUNRISE, ON JADE
MOUNTAIN, THE HIGHEST PEAK IN TAIWAN**

CPSIA information can be obtained
at www.ICGtesting.com
Printed in the USA
BVHW030051130322
631351BV00006B/267